THE ONLY SAFE PLACE IS ON THE RUN

THE ONLY SAFE PLACE IS ON THE RUN

SNOWDEN

JOSEPH GORDON-LEVITT // SHAILENE WOODLEY

// DIRECTED BY:
OLIVER STONE

// SCREENPLAY BY:
KIERAN FITZGERALD & OLIVER STONE

Skyhorse Publishing

Based upon the book *The Time of the Octopus* by Anatoly Kucherena
Based on *The Guardian* book by Luke Harding

Snowden film stills by Jürgen Olczyk. © 2016 Sacha, Inc. Courtesy of Open Road
Films, LLC.

Skyhorse Publishing books may be purchased in bulk at special discounts for
sales promotion, corporate gifts, fund-raising, or educational purposes. Special
editions can also be created to specifications. For details, contact the Special Sales
Department, Skyhorse Publishing, 307 West 36th Street, 11th Floor, New York,
NY 10018 or info@skyhorsepublishing.com.

Skyhorse® and Skyhorse Publishing® are registered trademarks of Skyhorse
Publishing, Inc.®, a Delaware corporation.

Visit our website at www.skyhorsepublishing.com.

10 9 8 7 6 5 4 3 2 1

Library of Congress Cataloging-in-Publication Data is available on file.

Cover design by Open Road Films and Brian Peterson
Cover art © 2016 Open Road Films. All rights reserved.

Print ISBN: 978-1-5107-1965-1
Ebook ISBN: 978-1-5107-1971-2

Printed in the United States of America

Foreword

Only a very rare individual would blow up his life for his principles, particularly a young, successful professional with his whole future in front of him. But that's precisely what twenty-nine-year-old Edward Snowden did in May 2013 when he left behind his life in Hawaii as an NSA computer wizard, including his longtime girlfriend Lindsay Mills, and flew to Hong Kong, where he handed over thousands of classified NSA documents to journalists Glenn Greenwald, Laura Poitras, and Ewen MacAskill. As soon as news stories based on the secret material—which revealed a massive global surveillance system that Orwell's Big Brother could only have dreamed about—began appearing in the *Guardian* and the *Washington Post*, Ed Snowden's old life was over. He became fugitive number one, relentlessly hunted by US security forces, which cut off his escape route to Latin America where he sought sanctuary and forced him to seek asylum in Russia.

To this day, Ed Snowden is a man without a country, a stranger in a strange land, in exile from his own homeland, which he had served throughout his young life as a US Army Special Forces candidate, CIA recruit, and NSA genius. And yet, accused of betraying his country, he remains one of the greatest patriots of his generation. No other young American has taken a braver stand in defense of our constitutional liberties.

To freedom-loving people in the United States and around the world—including many leaders and citizens of allied nations such as France, Germany, and Brazil, whom Snowden revealed to be the targets of US spying—the young whistle-blower was a new Paul Revere, attempting to wake up the public to the growing police state that looms over us. "We have sensors in our pockets that track us everywhere we go," Snowden warned. "A child born today [will] never know what it means to have a private moment to themselves, an unrecorded, unanalyzed thought. That's a problem because privacy matters; [it] allows us to determine who we are, and who we want to be."

There is something messianic about this precise and deliberate man. "If you seek to help," he wrote in an open letter as his eye-opening documents began to flutter around the world, "join the open source community and fight to keep the spirit of the press alive and the Internet free. I have been to the darkest corners of government, and what they fear is the light."

Snowden has had honors bestowed on him abroad, and the European Parliament has even called for amnesty on his behalf. At home he has become a civil liberties hero, and Pentagon Papers leaker Daniel Ellsberg has rightly credited him with sparking a process to roll back the authoritarian Patriot Act legislation passed in the United States after 9/11, an act of sacrificial bravery for which Snowden deserves a Nobel Peace Prize, according to Ellsberg.

Meanwhile, Snowden remains a dangerous villain in the eyes of America's powerful security complex—that sprawling intelligence empire that began proliferating like kudzu vines after 9/11, until it included hundreds of shadowy government agencies, hundreds more private security contractors, and an army of nearly one million employees who hold top-secret security clearances.

Ex-CIA director James Woolsey is among those who have called for Snowden's capture and execution. Following the Paris terror attacks in November 2015, which Woolsey through a tortured process tried to blame on the whistle-blower, the former CIA chief told CNN, "I would give [Snowden] the death sentence, and I would prefer to see him hanged by the neck until he's dead, rather than merely electrocuted."

These extreme sentiments in national security circles are why Ellsberg believes Ed Snowden will not be coming home any time soon. "I do not think he will ever be able to come back to the United States, no matter how popular he might come to be," Ellsberg told the *Guardian* during an overseas trip in 2015 that included a stopover in Moscow to visit with the young man who had followed in his footsteps. Ellsberg said he did not believe "the intelligence community will ever forgive him for having exposed what they were doing. I don't think any president will find it politic to confront the intelligence community by pardoning him or allowing him to come back."

And so Edward Snowden remains a shadow man, an avatar representing the great collision between the forces of security and freedom that continues to haunt the West. While flag-waving spooks and media pundits try to define Snowden in their own terms, as a traitor, a narcissist, a coward, and so on, the young whistle-blower has done a commendable job of defining himself, through documentaries like the Academy Award–winning *Citizenfour*, video speeches beamed into conferences, and television interviews. He comes across as an old soul, a deeply thoughtful young man wise beyond his years. But since Snowden is a creature of the computer world, there is something inevitably cerebral and remote about these electronic appearances.

Now, however, we have Oliver Stone's dramatic film *Snowden*, the most successful effort to fully present Snowden as a flesh-and-blood human being and not just a political symbol. It's the story of a young, patriotic man whose desire to serve his country after 9/11 ultimately runs headlong into the Orwellian realities he confronts about the new era. We've seen Stone wrestle before with this battle of conscience in a young American hero, most memorably with Ron Kovic, the broken soldier played by Tom Cruise in the searing *Born on the Fourth of July*. The filmmaker has a great feel for the disillusionment and soul-searching and the ultimate moment of no return that comes with this agonizing but ultimately liberating process. In the old days, we called it "radicalization." But in Snowden's case, perhaps it's more accurate to call it "enlightenment," the hacker's glow that comes from when you've finally connected the dots and you come to a higher level of understanding about how the world really works. This is the stuff of riveting political and psychological drama (and perhaps technological and spiritual as well).

For Snowden, it was a brutal and costly process, and Stone's film pulses with the terrors and thrills of this human evolution. But in the end, there was only one decision Snowden could make. It ended his brilliant career, it made him a wanted man, but now he can sleep in peace, knowing he did the right thing. The rest is up to us.

—David Talbot

Acknowledgments

For their generous and enduring support, the writers would like to thank the following people: Michael and Kathy Fitzgerald, Aidan Fitzgerald, Noah Gardner, and Janet Lee.

1.   **INT. ARCADE - MIRA HOTEL - HONG KONG #1 - MORNING**

SUPER: **The following is a dramatization of actual events that occurred between 2004 and 2013.**

Sliding to a reflection and then the physical back of a MAN in jeans and a white T-shirt standing at a rack of SD cards in an ELECTRONICS STORE. Customers around him ogle the latest digital toys.

CLOSE intense eyes staring through half-rimmed glasses.

Through the store window, we see a 10-foot-tall PLASTIC ALLIGATOR dressed in a tourist shirt that reads: I heart Hong Kong. Moving to a MAN seated close by on a bench facing away.

The man on the bench: journalist GLENN GREENWALD, 46, jacket and tie, sleepless for days. Running on adrenaline.

SUPER: **June 2013**

A woman comes and sits next to him--documentary filmmaker, LAURA POITRAS, 51. Equally frayed.

> GLENN

So?

> LAURA

This is the only alligator.

> GLENN (checking his watch)

Four minutes past. We walk in one minute--he was clear on that.

LAURA

He's coming.

Laura nods at a MAN in his 40s approaching down the arcade. They both search him out.

GLENN

No, he's too young to have that kind of access.

A BLUR of fingers and colors that becomes HANDS manipulating the sides of a RUBIK'S CUBE fast.

Laura is already looking past him, surprised. Glenn turns to see a young man of slight build with a porcelain pale boyish face and the shadow of a goatee--this is EDWARD SNOWDEN, 29.

CLOSE UP--the Rubik's cube turning in his hands, pulling focus to Glenn's eyes recognizing the signal. Glenn, standing, fumbles the pre-arranged greeting.

GLENN

So what time does the restaurant open?

SNOWDEN

Noon. But the food's a little too spicy.

Snowden's eyes flit up and down the arcade, tracking faces.

SNOWDEN

This way.

He turns, walks. Glenn and Laura collect their backpacks and follow him, exchanging looks.

2.   INT. ELEVATOR - MIRA HOTEL - MORNING

The three alone. Silence. Snowden offers a polite smile, nothing more...

At the 10th floor, the elevator dings, and he steps out...

3.   INT. HALLWAY - MIRA HOTEL - MORNING

...and walks briskly down a long dark maze-like CORRIDOR with mirrors extending the distances. The low seven-foot ceilings give it a cozy, closed labyrinthine effect. Snowden scans everything with casual vigilance.

At ROOM 1014, a 'Do Not Disturb' sign on the door. Pulling a key card from his wallet, he pauses, unused to letting anyone in. With a deep breath, he opens it.

4.   INT. SNOWDEN'S ROOM - MIRA HOTEL - MORNING

...and closes it as soon as Glenn and Laura are inside. A hint of a smile.

                    SNOWDEN
        It's really great to finally meet you guys.

Glenn and Laura start to answer.

                    SNOWDEN
        Sorry, but can I ask you first for your
        cell phones, please...?

Laura produces hers. Glenn hesitates.

                    SNOWDEN
        We want Laura to be the only one
        recording this, right?

Glenn gives him the cell. Snowden traverses the room--
ultra-modern in a modular style, small and littered with
empty take-out containers. He opens a MICROWAVE and
places both cell phones inside.

SNOWDEN (explaining)

I bought it to block radio frequencies.

Laura starts unloading the CAMERA GEAR from her
pack.

Glenn sits across from Snowden, composing himself.
Snowden is staring anxiously at Laura's camera. She
senses it's a personal demon for him.

LAURA

You've been photographed before, right?

SNOWDEN (clears his throat)

...Well, actually it's been a while since
anyone's taken a photo of me...

Laura glances at Glenn. Who is this guy?

LAURA

Try thinking of this as your friend. Take
your time.

GLENN

Can you start by telling us why you're
doing what you're doing? Give us some...

LAURA (slowing him down)

Glenn...(to Snowden) Let's start with
your name, OK?

LAURA'S CAMERA--Snowden turning back to Glenn. His face coming into focus--nervous, yet resolute. He breathes, and exuding a certain equanimity:

> SNOWDEN

My name is Edward Joseph Snowden...

5.   EXT. TRAINING GROUNDS - FORT BENNING, GEORGIA - PRE-DAWN

WIDE on a forest of tall pines in gray light.

SUPER: **Advanced Infantry Training, Georgia - 2004.**

> SNOWDEN (V.O.)
>
> I'm 29 years old. I work as a private contractor for the NSA. I've also worked as a private contractor for the CIA and directly for the Agency. I worked in various jobs in the intelligence industry for the last nine years. I've been a systems engineer, a solutions consultant, and a senior adviser for the Central Intelligence Agency.

Through the trees come two lines of ARMY TRAINEES-- 40 total. They carry 80-pound rucksacks and M16-A2 RIFLES...

CLOSE on the combat trainees, 18 to 30. Sweating buckets, ragged with exhaustion. They've been marching since 2 AM.

In the middle of the pack, wearing a pair of GI glasses, his expression determined at all costs, is PRIVATE SNOWDEN, 21.

CLOSE on his legs marching. They wobble a bit. A DRILL
SERGEANT comes jogging up the line.

                    DRILL SERGEANT

     So you pathetic sacks of shit want to be
     Special Forces?("Yes sir!" in chorus)
     Well I don't think so. I think Special
     Forces would be ashamed to call you
     soldiers. Am I right?

                ARMY TRAINEES (in unison)

     Sir, no, sir!

6.   EXT. OBSTACLE COURSE - DAY

CLOSE on combat boots RACING down mud tracks,
JUMPING onto logs. Hands SEIZING ropes and GROPING
for monkey bars.

SNOWDEN sprints towards a rope swing over mud, gets a
poor grip, lands hard on his side. He stumbles on, covered
with mud.

CLOSE on Snowden crawling up through a DRAIN PIPE
toward an opening. He hauls himself out and almost
collapses. The same DRILL SERGEANT gets in his face.

                    DRILL SERGEANT

     What is with you Snowden?

                       SNOWDEN

     Nothing, sir!

                    DRILL SERGEANT

     Where is your fucking heart!

SNOWDEN

Right here, sir! (pounds his heart area)

DRILL SERGEANT

Then show me your heart because I am your motherfucking heart detector!

SNOWDEN

Yes, sir!

DRILL SERGEANT

I want you to reach down there into that pathetic excuse of a chest and find your fucking heart Snowden! Now get your brokedick up that tower.

SNOWDEN

Yes, sir!

Snowden climbing a ladder--30 feet up. Really struggling now.

7.   INT. BARRACKS - EVENING

The MEN sleep in their bunks.

DRILL SERGEANT (V.O.)

Fallout! One minute outside!

They all shoot up as one to the command, out of their bunks and running.

Snowden slides to the edge of the bunk and jumps. But his feet are unable to take the weight and he crumbles to the floor, surprised! His mind is telling him one thing, but his body another.

Outside, his unit calls off their names. Anxious to catch up, he tries to get up--once, twice. Now he's scared, <u>nothing</u> is working. What's happening to him?

The Barrack is totally empty--silence. But he lies there like a flopping fish, alone. The surprise of it--questioning himself. His strength, his manhood.

SNOWDEN

> ...I'm hurt...Help. Help me!

Fear and pain envelop him.

8.   INT. ARMY HOSPITAL - FORT BENNING, GEORGIA - DAY (24 HOURS LATER)

Close on Snowden on drugs. An ARMY DOCTOR, 50s, appears to him other-worldly, displaying an MRI scan. TWO other PATIENTS share the room.

DOCTOR (Southern accent)

> You know you've been walking around on two broken legs? Best I can tell for weeks...

Snowden tries to move one leg and grimaces in pain, as we see the leg stabilized by metal rods; he feels a paralyzing bolt of pain.

DOCTOR

> Put an 80-pound ruck sack on a 130-pound body, little fractures build up in the tibias...And if you don't get off them, well eventually they bust. You'll be here a few weeks. And I'd count on another eight weeks or so on crutches.

                          SNOWDEN (blurry)

Can I go back then?

                          DOCTOR (sympathetic)

Son: you go back, ever, and you land
on those legs, airborne or not, your
bones'll turn to powder...(writing on his
clipboard) I'm gonna have to give you
an administrative discharge. (noticing
the shock on his face) Don't take it so
hard. Plenty of other ways to serve your
country.

TIME CUT -- NIGHT-- HOSPITAL - Snowden is on his
laptop when--DING, a chat window from a DATING
SITE appears on the desktop. JOURNEY_GIRL14 has
responded. Her message reads: **_Are you this pale in real_**
life? The gloom parts a little from his expression.

                    FEMALE VOICE (V.O.)

Have you ever committed a crime for
which you weren't caught?

9.   **INT. CIA HEADQUARTERS - LANGLEY,**
       VIRGINIA - DAY

CLOSE on two rubber tubes being affixed around
Snowden's torso...

                      SNOWDEN (V.O.)

      No.

                    FEMALE VOICE (V.O.)

Have you ever cheated on an exam?

CLOSE on a blood pressure cuff being wrapped around his arm...and galvanic sensors being fitted on two of his fingers.

> SNOWDEN (V.O.)
>
> Nope.

A POLYGRAPH ADMINISTRATOR looks up at Snowden seated before her in a windowless room, his sensors very calm.

> POLYGRAPH ADMINISTRATOR (female)
>
> Do you believe the United States is the greatest country in the world?

> SNOWDEN
>
> Yes.

She looks back down at the signal. Nothing out of the ordinary.

INTERCUT:

A SECOND ROOM at Langley. An INTERVIEWER sits across a desk from Snowden, who's in different clothing.

> INTERVIEWER
>
> Why do you want to join the CIA?

INTERCUT:

A THIRD ROOM. A PSYCHOLOGIST sits across from Snowden.

> PSYCHOLOGIST
>
> How would you explain the Internet to a child in one sentence?

INTERCUT:

A FOURTH ROOM--Snowden wears a rumpled jacket and tie at a table, warier.

A refined, sharp-eyed man sits opposite him, reading from his file in silence. This is a Senior Instructor at the CIA, CORBIN O'BRIAN, 50s.

> O'BRIAN
>
> Granddad--retired as an Admiral, then joined the FBI...? (impressed) Dad's in the Coast Guard--30-year man...

INTERCUT:

> PSYCHOLOGIST
>
> What's been the most important day in your life to date?

> SNOWDEN
>
> ...'9/11.' We thought my grandfather was inside the Pentagon. Turned out he was off-site that day.

INTERCUT:

> O'BRIAN
>
> You wanted to be Special Forces?

> SNOWDEN
>
> It was their motto, sir. *De Oppresso Liber.*

O'BRIAN

Is that what you hope to do with us?
Free people from oppression?

SNOWDEN

I'd like to help my country make a
difference in the world.

INTERCUT:

SNOWDEN (to Psychologist)

The Internet is a technology that has
the power to let everyone in the world
understand each other.

INTERCUT:

O'BRIAN

Missed a perfect score on the ASVAB
by a single question... Crushed their
language learning test...Some Japanese,
some Mandarin--(surprised) and no high
school diploma.

INTERCUT:

PSYCHOLOGIST

So why'd you stop attending high
school?

SNOWDEN

I had to make money. My parents were
divorcing at the time.

END INTERCUTTING

O'BRIAN

Any other influences?

SNOWDEN

I'd say Joseph Campbell. *Star Wars*.
Thoreau. Ayn Rand.

O'BRIAN

'One man can stop the motor of the
world.' Something like that? *Atlas
Shrugged*.

SNOWDEN

Yes, sir. I believe that.

O'BRIAN

Let's try again. Why do you want to join
the CIA?

SNOWDEN

Well, frankly, it's kinda 'cool' sir--to have
a top security clearance.

O'Brian smiles for the first time. He looks back at his file
and closes it.

O'BRIAN

It's not enough...

Snowden's face sinks.

O'BRIAN

...ordinarily. But these are not ordinary
times. Bombs won't wipe out terrorism.
Brains will. And we don't have nearly

enough of them. I'm going to give you a
shot.

Snowden stands offering his hand.

SNOWDEN

Thank you, sir. You won't regret this!

O'BRIAN

My name's Corbin O'Brian. I have many
titles, among them 'Senior Instructor.'
You'll be joining my class at 'The Hill.'

CUT TO:

10.   EXT. WARRENTON TRAINING CENTER, 'THE HILL' - VIRGINIA - DAY

THREE GERMAN SHEPHERDS on leashes sniff under and
around a beat-up Toyota. The CIA GUARDS guiding them
peer into the car. A FOURTH GUARD inspects the open
trunk.

Snowden in the driver's seat. The gate ahead opens. A
guard waves him on. He drives through barbed wire
FENCING...

11.   INT. CLASSROOM BUILDING - THE HILL - VIRGINIA - DAY

SUPER: **Warrenton Training Center, 'The Hill,' Virginia - 2006**

Snowden walks a HALL, checking door numbers. He spots
an open one, containing a mini-museum of sorts--radio
spyware, encryption machinery, and computers spanning
the 20th century...He's curious.

HANK

You'll be looking for Corbin's class.
End of the hall, keep going through the
second set of doors.

At his desk, his hands inside something that looks like a
1940s typewriter is HANK FORRESTER, 60s. A slightly
damaged, skittish look about him.

SNOWDEN

Thanks. Is that 'Enigma'?

HANK

No. Enigma was broken. That's a follow
up--the 'Sigaba'. Never broken. Cold
War's greatest encryption machine.
Tides of history ticked through those
rotors...(fixes a metal rotor in place) One
day everyone's gonna want a machine
like that.

SNOWDEN

I always wanted to learn cryptography.
What's this one?

HANK

The 'Hot Line.' First direct link between
Washington and Moscow. Probably
prevented WWIII. You got a name? How
do I know you're not the enemy?

SNOWDEN (realizing)

I'm sorry. Snowden, Ed Snowden.

HANK

Hank Forrester. Where'd you study,
Snowden?

SNOWDEN

I'm mostly self-taught...(noticing
another machine) You can tell me if
you're busy, but is that a 'Cray-1'?

HANK (proudly)

Yes. The first super computer. Can get all
this on a cell phone now.

SNOWDEN

So you're an engineer?

HANK

Instructor and counselor too. I'm
supposed to keep an eye on you CTs, see
you don't buckle under the pressure--
turn to drugs and booze.

SNOWDEN

You won't have that problem with me. I
don't drink or do drugs.

HANK

So, what's your sin of choice?

SNOWDEN

Computers.

HANK

Well then Snowden, you've come to the
right little whorehouse.

12.   INT. CLASSROOM - THE HILL - VIRGINIA - DAY

Twelve CIA TRAINEES, most in their 20s, a few over
30, two females among them. They don't look rough
enough for the military--each person with a DESKTOP
and a TOWER SERVER-- each desk labeled neatly as an
international city. One trainee is a token military man,
40s, buzzcut.

At the front, O'Brian paces through the light of a
projector displaying logs from the 'cities' on a screen
behind him. It's a special classroom with built-in screens,
microphones dangling from the ceiling.

TALL RACKS of 10–12 SERVERS, eight feet high, stretch
along the walls into a back room in an impressive display
of computing power.

> O'BRIAN
>
> ...The front lines in the Global War on
> Terror are not in Iraq, or Afghanistan.

O'Brian comes to the first desk, lays his hand on a server.

> O'BRIAN
>
> They're here. In London. Berlin...

O'Brian continues down the class, touching servers.

> O'BRIAN
>
> ...in Istanbul. Lagos. Manila. Any server,
> any connection, anywhere. All the time.
> Which means you don't have to sit in a
> ditch eating MREs and looking out for
> mortar fire. It means, that if there is
> another 9/11,' it'll be your fault. Just as
> the first one was our generation's, take

my word for it, you do not want to live
with that burden.

CLOSE on the solemn faces of the Trainees. Snowden at
the Buenos Aires desk, following intensely.

O'BRIAN (V.O.)

We're going to start with an Aptitude
Test. See where you are. Each of you is
going to build a covert communications
site in your home city.

TIME CUT -- MONTAGE of TRAINEES typing furiously /
jogging up to the servers / pulling out the back walls and
repatching cable.

O'BRIAN (V.O.)

You're going to deploy, back up your
site, destroy it, and restore it again. The
point of this exercise is to keep your
infrastructure up and running securely.
The average test time is five hours. If
you take more than eight, you will fail.

CLOSE on Snowden at his desktop, typing, concentrated.

O'BRIAN

Your hours start now.

TIME CUT -- Snowden pushes his chair back. He heads to
the front where O'Brian works at a laptop. A MONITOR
watches the class.

SNOWDEN

Mr. O'Brian, I'm done, sir.

O'BRIAN

You don't have to tell me when you've
completed a stage...

SNOWDEN

No, I finished the whole thing.

O'BRIAN (taken aback)

It's been 40 minutes.

SNOWDEN

Thirty-eight.

O'BRIAN

Okay, let's go see where you screwed up.

O'Brian, irritated, walks down the rows of desks with
Snowden following. He sits in his seat, begins typing.

O'Brian drifts off as he inspects the work. He stops
typing. He's not a man easily stunned, but right now he's
stupefied.

SNOWDEN

You didn't say we had to do it in order,
sir. I broke the 'sequence' to save time
and automated the back-up to run as I
built the site...

The sound of typing has stopped. All heads are turned.

O'BRIAN

Eyes on screens.

Trainees' heads whip round, fingers flying again. O'Brian
starts back toward the front.

SNOWDEN

Sir? What should I do now?

O'BRIAN

Whatever you want.

Snowden grabs his bag, heads for the door, receiving cold looks. His mind is already miles away...

13.   INT. COFFEE SHOP - WASHINGTON D.C. - DAY

Ed's POV: locking on one female face after another.

Anxiously, he sits in a corner, his gaze hovering above his open laptop on the door. As disappointment sets in, his eye catches on a reflection in his screen.

He turns to catch a trim, athletic girl with a warm smile and lively eyes, LINDSAY MILLS, 20--snapping a picture of him with a Nikon. She waves briskly, heading in.

He stands as she approaches. Although sizing him up boldly, she's not quite secure.

ED

Hi.

LINDSAY

Yup. Let's get you some sun.

14.   EXT. NATIONAL MALL - WASHINGTON D.C. - DAY

CLOSE as Lindsay SNAPS photos of Ed, standing against an elm tree; she seems to use the camera as a screen between them.

ED

Sorry it took me this long. You didn't
want to see me on crutches. I wasn't so
agile. And then this new job hit.

LINDSAY

What was it you're going to be doing
again?

ED

Analysis for the State Department.

LINDSAY

Can you do me a favor: point in the
direction of the State Department.

Ed scans the mall: TOURISTS, FAMILIES having picnics,
enjoying the sunny autumn day...He nods generally
toward the Washington Monument.

ED

It's over there.

LINDSAY

You sure?

ED

I'm not great at orienting myself.

LINDSAY

You're not that great at lying either.
You'll have to work on both if you're
going to be a spy.

He's caught completely off guard.

LINDSAY

Where I grew up, everyone's parents
worked for the...
　　(with quotation fingers)
...*State Department.* Plus every time you
visited my website this week, which was
often, it was from an IP in Virginia.

ED (surprised)

You know how to run IP traces?

LINDSAY

My dad taught me how to keep track
of my customers. And I'm pretty sure
the State Department has no offices in
Virginia.

She smiles, eyes sparkling. Ed is smitten. Lindsay walks
away, then spins around, and points the camera at him.

LINDSAY

Come on. Let's see you strut it.

Ed does his best 'catwalk' towards her. He looks very
uncomfortable. Lindsay laughs as she takes photos.

TIME CUT -- They carry on down the Mall, passing
BOOTHS and POLITICAL ACTIVISTS with signs--Vietnam
Veterans' MIA, American Indians, Environmental
Movement...

Lindsay stops at a booth with Iraqi War protest
materials-- "Not in Our Name," "No To War," "Drop Bush/
Not Bombs," a US flag with corporations listed in the

blue part of the flag. She signs a petition and tracks Ed's reaction. He looks uncomfortable.

> LINDSAY
>
> Too much independent spirit for you?

> ED
>
> I'm just not into bashing my country.

> LINDSAY
>
> It's my country too, and right now it has blood on its hands.

> ED
>
> Sorry: I have friends who are over there right now.

> LINDSAY
>
> I'm not talking about the troops. I'm talking about the moron sending them to war.

> ED
>
> You mean our commander-in-chief.

> LINDSAY
>
> Yeah...Well, whatever you want to call him: he's wrong.

> ED
>
> How do you know he's wrong? You're just lashing out.

LINDSAY

No, I'm not lashing out, I'm questioning our government. That's what we do in this country. That's the principle we were founded on.

ED

What about questioning the liberal media? You're still buying what one side is saying.

LINDSAY

Maybe I am. Cause my side is right.

ED

Funny, so is mine.

LINDSAY

Why is it smart conservatives make me so mad?

ED

Probably because you don't like hearing the truth.

LINDSAY

You are a very frustrating individual, you know that? How am I going to make you see?

ED

I can see just fine, thanks.

She eyes him and then takes his face and KISSES him.
He's too startled to react. She pulls back, assessing her
work--Ed glows.

> ### LINDSAY
>
> That help at all?

He walks on, wiping his mouth in faux-disgust.

> ### ED
>
> No, that did nothing for me. Tastes like
> 'liberal.' Not my thing.

They laugh. They have <u>something</u>, not sure, in common.

15.   INT. CLASSROOM - THE HILL - VIRGINIA - DAY

O'Brian holds up a newspaper in front of the class with a
blaring headline:

> ### O'BRIAN
>
> *New York Times* last week. Front page.
>   (reading)
> *"Bush Lets US Spy On Callers Without
> Courts."* Is it constitutional to bypass the
> Courts?

MARTIN, 24, at the Rio server blurts out:

> ### MARTIN
>
> No. The Fourth Amendment prevents
> searches and seizures without a
> warrant.

> ### O'BRIAN
>
> That's absolutely right, 'Rio'. Which
> means your Commander-in-Chief,

the President of the United States, is
breaking the law. That is what you're
saying, isn't it, 'Rio'?

Martin shifts uncomfortably under O'Brian's gaze.

MARTIN

Well...I guess it depends...on who you
talk to...

Close on Snowden typing in the back at the Mexico City
station with a hint of a smile.

O'BRIAN

And if you talk to journalists...? (holding
up the newspaper)...Who, more often
than not, don't have the full picture...or
neglect to report it, then you only get a
partial truth.

O'Brian goes to a whiteboard, writes: FISA Court.

O'BRIAN

Foreign Intelligence Surveillance Act,
the FISA Court. We do respect the Fourth
Amendment in this country and we
issue warrants based on suspicion. But
sometimes these warrants have to be
issued by secret courts so that we do not
alert the suspects we're spying on. And
these court proceedings are classified,
which means, surprise!--they're not
included in papers such as the *New York
Times*.

16. INT. HANK'S MUSEUM/OFFICE - THE HILL - DAY

Hank goes to a glass case, unlocks it, and takes down a framed photo from the top shelf.

SNOWDEN

Have you seen my test scores?

HANK (ominously)

Yes, I have.

He shows Snowden the photo: *20 YOUNG MEN with crew cuts standing in two rows.*

HANK (points to a face)

Top of my class. Like you.

SNOWDEN

Here?

HANK

NSA. They liked me plenty. Put me on the best teams. Soviet frontier. Desert Storm. And then the big new challenge: finding the terrorist in the Internet haystack. Hell of a haystack--hundreds of terrabytes a minute. Take you four hundred years to read the emails. Then you have to analyze them. Sometimes, the more you look, the less you see.

SNOWDEN

What'd you come up with?

> ### HANK
>
> It was a beauty--*in house* for three
> million bucks--a program that could
> differentiate between foreign and
> domestic, encrypt every signal we
> weren't targeting so it would stay
> private. Best work I ever did.

He returns the photo to its shelf.

> ### SNOWDEN
>
> What was it called?

> ### HANK (ignoring the question)
>
> Rising to the top in our world, Ed...can
> be hard on a man. You think you're
> making strides, taking the initiative.
> Next minute they grind your work out of
> existence.

> ### SNOWDEN
>
> They didn't use it? Why not?

> ### HANK
>
> Oh, they never tell you why...Two years
> later, after 9/11, a friend of mine tells
> me about this new contractor program
> they're using. Costs <u>four billion</u> dollars
> to deploy. Modeled after mine but with
> no filters, no automation. Ingested
> everything. They were drowning in data.
> Frickin' disaster.

SNOWDEN

That much money? There's got to be a bigger picture...I mean, they're not stupid.

HANK

You'd think intelligence would count for something in the intelligence business...You want to know what it is? What really sets the agenda? *Military Industrial Happiness Management.* Keep the coffers open in Congress, the money flowing to contractors. Efficiency, results--they go out the window. Not to mention...

Hank stops himself.

HANK

You're late for class.

Snowden lingers at the door.

SNOWDEN

Did you ever try and do something?

HANK

Sure. We went to legal. Filed complaints. Here I am, tucked away teaching you. Maybe that's more important in the long run.

Hank nods at the Rubik's cube spinning in Ed's hand.

HANK

Getting better.

17.   EXT. WOODED HILLSIDE - VIRGINIA - LATE DAY

Snowden and O'Brian in winter jackets ascend a path up the SNOW-COVERED hill. They reach a clearing, looking out.

> **O'BRIAN**
>
> My favorite spot on campus...You hunt, Ed?

> **SNOWDEN**
>
> I used to go skeet shooting with my Dad. Never hunted.

> **O'BRIAN**
>
> We'll go one day.

He has something to say, hesitates. Snowden clears his throat. O'Brian has become a mentor to him but remains a formidable presence.

> **SNOWDEN**
>
> Can I ask you a question, Mr. O'Brian?

> **O'BRIAN**
>
> How about just calling me Corbin.

> **SNOWDEN**
>
> Well, I was talking with Hank Forrester and...I was wondering: are all our SIGINT programs specifically targeted?

O'BRIAN

Of course, what good would they be if
they weren't?
(holding his gaze)
Do you have a girlfriend, Ed?

SNOWDEN

Nothing serious.

O'BRIAN

What's her name?

SNOWDEN

Lindsay.

O'BRIAN

Will she be going with you?

SNOWDEN

I don't want to put her in any kind of
danger.

O'BRIAN

You won't have to. We're not sending you
to the Middle East.

SNOWDEN (stunned)

Sir, I'm your best student. Doesn't that
count for something...?

Snowden doesn't understand.

O'BRIAN

In 20 years, Iraq will be a hellhole nobody
cares about. Terrorism's a short-term

threat. The real threats will come from
China, Russia, Iran, and they'll come as
SQL injections and malware. Without
minds like yours, this country will be
picked apart in cyberspace. I'm not
going to risk losing you to a horseshit
war over sand and oil.

SNOWDEN

I'm surprised to hear you say that.

O'BRIAN

You don't have to agree with your
politicians to be a patriot.

His cell buzzes. He claps Snowden on the shoulder.

SNOWDEN

Sir, where are you sending me?

O'BRIAN

Take a moment. Enjoy the view.

He turns and walks back down, the cell to his ear.
Snowden is left standing alone.

18.   INT. SNOWDEN'S ROOM - MIRA HOTEL - HONG
KONG #2A - NIGHT

Glenn knocks at 'Room 1014.' Laura opens. Glenn stands
with EWEN MACASKILL, 60s, a seasoned Scottish
political correspondent with London's *Guardian*
newspaper, for whom Glenn freelances. Seeing Ewen,
Laura goes cold. They enter to find Snowden pacing.

EWEN

...Ewen MacAskill from the *Guardian*.
Pleased to meet you.

Snowden shakes his hand. Ewen takes out his cell.

EWEN

If you don't mind, I'd like to record our...

Snowden walks away in disbelief. Laura takes Ewen's cell
and puts it in the microwave.

LAURA (bristling)

Cell phones go in the microwave.

EWEN

Dare I ask why?

LAURA

We'll get to that. After you ask your
questions.

EWEN

(reacting, sits opposite Snowden) Yes--
well, before we can move on any stories,
I've got to know more about you.

Snowden doesn't have time for this. He goes to his
backpack in the closet, rifles through it. Ewen pushes on:

EWEN

Your career, by Glenn's account, is
wide-ranging. But the *Guardian* needs
evidence that...

Snowden plants a stack of PERSONAL DOCUMENTS on
the bed. As he hands each one to Ewen, inundating him
with material:

SNOWDEN

Black diplomatic passport for friendly
countries, blue tourist for everywhere
else. Check the visa stamps. Driver's
License, my NSA badge with Booz
Allen, my CIA badge with Dell, my DIA
instructor badge...A photo of me and
Michael Hayden, former head of NSA
and CIA.

Ewen looks at the PHOTO: Hayden shaking hands with
Snowden at a black-tie event.

SNOWDEN

When can you publish?

EWEN

Glenn says you intend to reveal your
identity? How do you expect your
government'll react?

SNOWDEN

They'll charge me under the Espionage
Act. They'll say I endangered national
security. They'll demonize me, and my
friends and family, and they'll throw me
in jail. That's the best-case scenario.

EWEN

And the worst?

SNOWDEN

If I don't have any media cover, I'll be
rendered by the CIA and interrogated
outside the law. They have a station
right up the street.

EWEN

How would they know what you did?

SNOWDEN

Because I left a digital footprint in my
logs. They'll eventually figure it out. I
didn't want a manhunt. I know what
they'd do to my colleagues...

Their looks express their befuddlement.

SNOWDEN

I'm not in this for money or anything,
Mr. MacAskill. There's no hidden agenda
here. My plan was for you journalists
to present this to the world and let
the <u>people</u> decide: either I'm wrong, or
there's something happening inside our
government that's <u>really wrong</u>.

Snowden now produces an SD MEMORY CARD and hands
it to Ewen.

SNOWDEN

This one is everything I have on your
British intelligence agency, GCHQ. An
encryption key will follow. You'll want
your technical people at the *Guardian*
to go through it thoroughly. There's...a
lot of stuff there.

Ewen stares at the SD card. His face a shade graver.
He pockets the card and shares a look with Laura and
Glenn--they've received documents already and know the
procedure.

> SNOWDEN
>
> Listen: pretty soon they're going to
> investigate; they're going to figure out
> what I've done, they're going to come for
> me. And now that we've made contact
> they'll come for all of you too.

> EWEN
>
> May I go to the microwave for a
> moment?

19.   INT. GUARDIAN US OFFICES - NEW YORK CITY - DAY

JANINE GIBSON, 40s, editor of the *Guardian US*, leans
over the shoulder of a STAFF EDITOR, checking copy.

A wooden floor in a downtown loft--25 EMPLOYEES. Her
cell BUZZES. She checks the number. Stiffens.

20.   EXT. MIRA HOTEL - HONG KONG - NIGHT

Ewen walking in a sea of Asian faces on a crowded
shopping street, phone to his ear.

> EWEN
>
> Janine?

Janine enters her office, putting the call in conference
mode for her deputy editor, STUART MILLAR, 40s.

JANINE

Ewen?...I'm on with Stuart.

EWEN (with a smile)

Well, all I can say is--'the Guinness here
is good.'

JANINE

Wonderful!

TIME CUT -- She hangs up, looks at Stuart. Exhilarated
and nervous, they both know what this entails.

JANINE

So, now we have the lawyers to deal
with. And no doubt the White House.

**21.   INT. SNOWDEN'S ROOM - MIRA HOTEL - HONG
          KONG #2B - NIGHT**

Ewen returns his cell to the microwave, turning to the
three expectant faces...

EWEN

OK. I've got the go-ahead.

GLENN

Good. We've got a lot get through here
and it's not easy reading.

LAURA

We can start by showing him XKeyscore.

GLENN

Yes--XKeyscore. Good idea. (to Ed) Can
you pull it up and take us through it
again?

Snowden hoods himself and the laptop with a blanket,
starts typing.

EWEN (puzzled)

Do we all get under there now?

LAURA

He's protecting his passwords.

Snowden removes the blanket, waves them over.

SNOWDEN

This was introduced during my first
deployment at the CIA in Geneva.

EWEN

(reading off the laptop) *XKeyscore* What
does that do?

SNOWDEN

It's like a search interface.

EWEN

What does it search for?

CLOSE on Snowden, his eyes twinkling a little.

SNOWDEN

Anything you want.

22.   EXT. STREETS - GENEVA - DAY

DIGITAL 'CHIP TUNES' climb over the sound of traffic, as overhead camera follows a DRIVER, with a shoulder bag, through narrow, clean streets. In the distance across LAKE GENEVA, the foothills of the Alps are visible.

> EWEN (V.O.)
>
> What was your assignment in Geneva?

> SNOWDEN (V.O.)
>
> I was assigned with diplomatic cover to the UN Mission to maintain the CIA's computer security network.

REVERSE on the Driver: Snowden, in an office jacket with earbud wires poking out from his helmet, nods to the beat.

> SNOWDEN (V.O.)
>
> I had spent almost two years around CIA field officers.

23.   EXT. US DIPLOMATIC MISSION - GENEVA - DAY

Snowden pulls up to a GUARDHOUSE. A metal gate slides open. He drives through, headed toward: A SEVEN-STORY BUILDING with solar panels and satellite dishes on the roof.

SUPER: **US DIPLOMATIC MISSION, GENEVA - 2008**

24. INT. CIA STATION - TOP FLOOR - US MISSION - GENEVA - DAY

Snowden, in disbelief, follows his boss, KEVIN DAVINI, 40s/50s, a dour, authoritarian expression, into his office.

> SNOWDEN
>
> I'm sorry, sir. I don't understand.

> KEVIN
>
> Sherman says you 'hacked' the Human Resources site.

> SNOWDEN
>
> My job is to find flaws.

> KEVIN
>
> The security of the HR site is not your problem. You went outside the wheelhouse.

As he enters his office space.

> SNOWDEN
>
> I didn't hack it. I showed it could be hacked and you told me to patch it.

> KEVIN
>
> Do you have that in writing?

> SNOWDEN
>
> Yes, I do. And I gave you proof of concept.

KEVIN (surprised)

It doesn't matter what you did,
Snowden. Right or wrong, you need
to let these things be someone else's
problem. He's also put a derog in your
file.

SNOWDEN

Excuse me?!

KEVIN

Let it be a lesson. I don't want him
calling me again about another 'Ed
Snowden moment,' okay?

Snowden is silent. Incredulous.

KEVIN (by way of sympathy)

Take it easy the rest of the day. Go work
on the scrubbing pile.

As Snowden goes back to the floor, passing MATT KOVAR,
37, handsome, well-built, CIA field agent. Friend and role
model to Snowden.

MATT

That didn't look like it went well.

SNOWDEN

Can you believe it? I just got a derog for
doing my job.

MATT

Politics man. Culture of fear wins again.

SNOWDEN

I can't get anything done here. What
about that idea we talked about...?

MATT (cutting him off)

I'm working on it. I'm waiting on a call
back from our friend at 'The Hill.'

SNOWDEN (excited)

You called Corbin? You think he can
make something happen?

MATT

We'll see. Maybe limited field ops, under
my supervision.

SNOWDEN

Matt, anything! Please--

MATT

Easy, Ed. I have to go see a cleric in
Milan. We'll talk after.

25.   INT. GRINDING ROOM/ABCD ROOM - US MISSION - GENEVA - DAY

BUZZING. Snowden places a CD into a GRINDER
('grinding' destroys data). Wearing a surgical mask
for the dust, he takes out his frustration on one CD of
hundreds on a shelf.

A KNOCKING on the wall close to Snowden's head.
Snowden turns, startled.

Before him is: GABRIEL SOL, 20s/30s, puckish eyes, dyed hair, t-shirt. Snowden turns off the grinder, removes his mask.

GABRIEL

CIA does not like to leave a trace, huh?...

SNOWDEN

Can I help you?

GABRIEL (picking up a CD)

You ever get curious to check one out? See what kind of crazy-ass covert kill mission you might be erasing from history?

Snowden takes the CD from him.

SNOWDEN (dubiously)

Who are you with?

Gabriel displays an NSA BADGE, arching his brow in spy stereotype, whispering:

GABRIEL

'No Such Agency'. I'm "Gabriel Sol." I'm the 'Fifty Pound Brain' from the Council of Wizards and Warlocks--and I'm here to give you your intel for Bucharest.

Gabriel points to Snowden's badge. It reads: *Dave Churchyard.*

GABRIEL

Unless there's another 'Dave Churchyard'?

SNOWDEN

No, that's me. This way.

Snowden takes Gabriel across a partition into a small crowded, high-tech space where every secure network can be accessed. This is the computer brain of the mission. Snowden points to FOUR MONITORS.

SNOWDEN

I'll be right outside.

GABRIEL

Stay if you want.

SNOWDEN

I don't have authorization to use NSA programs.

GABRIEL

If you're the messenger to Bucharest, you must have a PRIVAC clearance to see the finished intel, yes? (Snowden nods) So what difference does it make if you see how it's put together? Up to you.

Snowden, tempted, hesitates. This would be the first time he's ever broken a USG rule--albeit a minor one.

SNOWDEN

Will you be giving me names?

GABRIEL

I've got a lot more than names.

Snowden pulls up a chair, his curiosity too much to overcome.

GABRIEL

What I will be providing you, and the
fine gentlemen of the Secret Service, is a
list...

Gabriel starts typing KEYWORDS into a program window.
We recognize the logo: *XKEYSCORE*.

GABRIEL

...of every threat made about the
president since February 3rd, and a
profile of every threat-maker.

SNOWDEN

You're pulling up...existing targets?

GABRIEL

Ninety-nine percent are going to come
from the bulk collection programs.
Upstream, Tempora, Muscular, Prism.

SNOWDEN

Prism?

Gabriel glances at the blank-faced Snowden.

GABRIEL

You got a little Snow White in you. Which
makes me feel like the witch bringing
you a poisoned apple.

Gabriel hits *return*. A list of emails, SMS messages, chats,
and online profiles starts automatically compiling in a
second window. Gabriel clicks on the first EMAIL in the
list.

                              GABRIEL

Exhibit A: Oakland resident Justin
Pinsky posted on a message board:
*Romania has a storied history of
executing their leaders, couldn't they do
us a solid and take out Bush?*

Gabriel clicks on a second piece of text.

                              GABRIEL

Oooo, this looks juicy. From a g-chat
between Lester Nash of Kansas City and
a Romanian wives service: *When I get to
Bucharest I'm going to attack your bush
with the biggest python you've ever seen.*

Gabriel chuckles. This is all completely normal for him.

                              SNOWDEN

How is this possible?

                              GABRIEL

'Attack,' 'take out,' 'Bush.' (pointing to
the keywords he typed in) Keyword
selectors.

Snowden is failing to wrap his head around this.

                              GABRIEL

Think of it as a Google search. But
instead of searching only what people
make public, we're also looking at
everything they don't--emails, chats,
SMS, whatever.

SNOWDEN

Which people?

GABRIEL

The whole kingdom, Snow White.

Gabriel amused by the expression on Snowden's face.

26.   EXT. AMBASSADOR'S RESIDENCE - GENEVA - DAY

A woman, bare-shouldered, walks alongside Snowden, in jacket/khakis, up a gravel path to a neoclassical home. The entrance is flanked by BUTLERS. OTHER GUESTS arriving at the same time. It takes a moment to recognize Lindsay.

LINDSAY

Which Ambassador was he?

SNOWDEN

De La Hoya, World Trade Organization.

27.   INT. AMBASSADOR'S RESIDENCE - GENEVA - DAY

Matt orders a drink, turns back: a glint in his eye:

MATT

O'Brian came through for you. He agrees your talents are being wasted. You ready for a little action?

SNOWDEN

Really? Here?

MATT

Yeah now, see the woman in the pink
number? Credit Suisse.

Snowden glances over at the BLONDE WOMAN. He picks
the other characters as Matt lists them:

MATT

JP Morgan is on her arm. Chunky's with
Deutsche Bank. Ten thousand bankers
in this town--all you need to turn is one.
Socialize. Meet a few. Preferably one
sitting on a pile of dirty Saudi money
that's funding Bin Laden.

EXT. GARDEN -- TIME CUTS -- A MONTAGE of Snowden
attempting to chat up GUESTS with little success. He's
inherently antisocial, and these people are veterans of
the Geneva scene--not easily drawn in.

We don't hear much dialogue, but we see eyes losing
interest in him, or becoming suspect. In each case, the
guest moves on.

Snowden is upset. His first opportunity to accomplish
field work is going nowhere fast.

TIME CUT -- Snowden is with Lindsay in another part of
the mansion, his expression hangdog with failure.

SNOWDEN

An Ambassador...wow. I wish I had your
schmoozing skills.

LINDSAY

Well, that's why you have me.

SNOWDEN

You don't know any bankers do you?

LINDSAY

Bankers? Are you on some kind of
assignment or something?

SNOWDEN

'Relationship cultivating.' And not well.

LINDSAY

Let me help you.

SNOWDEN

This is serious.

LINDSAY

I know it's serious. Trust me.

Before he can stop her, Lindsay melts into the crowd.

CUT TO:

Snowden finds Matt at the outdoor bar drinking alone.

MATT

Any luck?

Snowden shakes his head. Matt watches the woman from
before, she's with another man now.

SNOWDEN

No, no bites. Is there some trick to it?

MATT

It's all about finding the pressure point.
Everything else is just pushing on it.
(nodding across the crowd) Looks like
you're being summoned.

Snowden sees Lindsay, waving at him to hurry. He heads
over to find her with: MARWAN AL-KIRMANI, late
40s/50s, plump, sweet smile, charming British/Pakistani
accent. As he shakes hands with Snowden:

LINDSAY

Marwan, this is my boyfriend, Dave.

MARWAN

It's a pleasure.

LINDSAY

Marwan works at Monfort.

Snowden's unsure of his next move. Lindsay's way ahead
of him:

LINDSAY

We were talking and after last week, he
may be able to give you some tips.

Snowden has no idea what she's talking about.

SNOWDEN

Last week...?

LINDSAY (to Marwan)

He's embarrassed, it was a lot of money
for us.

MARWAN

Day-trading is a perilous sport. You shouldn't be ashamed of it.

LINDSAY

I'm going to grab some food. I'll see you guys inside?

Lindsay leaves them.

MARWAN

You have a lovely girlfriend.

SNOWDEN

Thank you. I work IT for the Embassy. Figured I could crack the market like it was a weak network.

MARWAN

May I ask how precipitous were your losses?

SNOWDEN

I told Lindsay it was 20,000. But between you and me, it was closer to 45. I tried to recoup but that was a mistake. Now without any real grounding I feel like I'm sliding out of control.

MARWAN

I have seen it many times, and I'm always happy to help a man break a bad habit before it gets going.

SNOWDEN

Thank you. I really appreciate that.

They walk together continuing to talk.

28.   INT. ABCD ROOM - US MISSION - GENEVA - THAT NIGHT

CLOSE on Gabriel, scanning text in the glow of a monitor.

GABRIEL

This is the cleanest Pakistani I've ever seen.

Snowden hovers behind him.

GABRIEL

No first degree ties to government or ISI. No shady family. Second degree contacts are off the charts, but that's everyone in the Middle East with a six-figure income.

SNOWDEN

We don't need dirt necessarily... We need a pressure point. (Gabriel types) Something intimate. Some weakness. Can we look through family members?

Gabriel is already scrolling through online IP addresses of computers belonging to Marwan's family.

GABRIEL

How about...his sister-in-law?

Gabriel types. Quickly opens a video. A stationary POV of a tidy bedroom. A PAKISTANI WOMAN in a burka sits on the bed taking her shoes off.

SNOWDEN

She sent this to someone?

GABRIEL

No, this is live. Out of...(checking the
feed) Paris.

Snowden's mind is blown again. Gabriel can tell.

GABRIEL

Optic Nerve. Camera and mike
activation. Wish we could take credit but
the Brits wrote it.

SNOWDEN

Activation?

GABRIEL

Her laptop's off. Or it was. She just forgot
to close it. Of course, how would she
know? This shit is so sly the webcam
light doesn't even turn on.

The woman takes the burka off. Revealing jeans and a
T-shirt.

GABRIEL

I always wondered what was under
those things...

SNOWDEN (disturbed)

Let's stick to family in Geneva.

GABRIEL

OK, Snow White.

GABRIEL (scanning profiles)

Wife. No employment. Fifteen-year-old
daughter at the International school.

SNOWDEN

Facebook. Is that...possible?

GABRIEL

Facebook's my bitch.

SNOWDEN

Fights with her parents, or--

GABRIEL

Don't worry. I know all the hooks for this
kind of fishing.

BRIEF SHOTS of Gabriel entering KEYWORDS into
XKeyscore: *boyfriend, girlfriend, sexy, love, luv, DTF.*

Snowden paces. Glancing every few seconds at Gabriel's
screen, then ripping his eyes away.

Snowden leans in as he points at the first text box:

GABRIEL

Query name. Email, keyword, whatever
selector you want...

Pointing to the second which reads: *Justification.*

GABRIEL

...and that's where I write...

Gabriel types: "*Associated with known facilitators of
Saudi finance.*" And continues his query.

Edward Snowden (Joseph Gordon-Levitt) in basic training for the US Army Special Forces.
Photo credit: Jürgen Olczyk

Edward Snowden (Joseph Gordon-Levitt, left) undergoes testing for his CIA security clearance.
Photo credit: Jürgen Olczyk

Edward Snowden (Joseph Gordon-Levitt, center) at the CIA training center in Virginia—"The Hill."
Photo credit: Jürgen Olczyk

(Left to right) Gabriel Sol (Ben Schnetzer) meets Edward Snowden (Joseph Gordon-Levitt) at the US Diplomatic Mission to the UN in Geneva, Switzerland. **Photo credit:** Jürgen Olczyk

(Left to right) Edward Snowden (Joseph Gordon-Levitt) learns about NSA surveillance from Gabriel Sol (Ben Schnetzer) at the US Diplomatic Mission to the UN in Geneva, Switzerland. **Photo credit:** Jürgen Olczyk

(Left to right) Edward Snowden (Joseph Gordon-Levitt) and Lindsay Mills (Shailene Woodley) at their apartment in Geneva, Switzerland. **Photo credit:** Jürgen Olczyk

CIA instructor Corbin O'Brian (Rhys Ifans) trains new hires.
Photo credit: Jürgen Olczyk

Edward Snowden (Joseph Gordon-Levitt) at a CIA training center.
Photo credit: Jürgen Olczyk

(Left to right) Edward Snowden (Joseph Gordon-Levitt) and Hank Forrester (Nicolas Cage) at a CIA training center. **Photo credit:** Jürgen Olczyk

(Left to right) Corbin O'Brian (Rhys Ifans) and Edward Snowden (Joseph Gordon-Levitt) hunting in Maryland. **Photo credit:** Jürgen Olczyk

Corbin O'Brian (Rhys Ifans) takes an important phone call.
Photo credit: Jürgen Olczyk

Edward Snowden (Joseph Gordon-Levitt, right) working as an NSA contractor in Japan.
Photo credit: Jürgen Olczyk

(Left to right) Corbin O'Brian (Rhys Ifans) has a video conference with Edward Snowden (Joseph Gordon-Levitt). **Photo credit:** Jürgen Olczyk

GABRIEL

...In other words, I'm turning your
Daddy into a CIA informant!

SNOWDEN

That's it?

GABRIEL

That's it, bro.

SNOWDEN

No...FISA court order?

GABRIEL

Not here. XKEYSCORE is under 702
authority, which means no warrants.

SNOWDEN

What about US targets? Don't we need a
court order?

GABRIEL

You mean FISA? They're just a big-
ass rubber stamp. FISA judges are all
appointed by the chief justice, who's like
you know, Darth Vader when it comes to
'national security.'

Snowden backs away, lost in thought, remembering all
that O'Brian told him, all that he didn't...Gabriel's fingers
pause on the keyboard.

GABRIEL

Boom! Here you go...

Gabriel points to a highlighted Facebook MESSAGE under a photo of SALMA, 15, Marwan's daughter. It reads: *I've been dreaming about his fingers. I think I'm ready*

> GABRIEL
>
> The boy at third base is...

Gabriel pulls up a photo of NADIME.

> GABRIEL
>
> ...Nadime. He's eighteen. Salma says she wants to marry him but is scared of telling her parents. What she doesn't know is that...

Gabriel pulls up a second Facebook profile page of "Nicolas" (aka Nadime) and photos of TWO GIRLS, 16 and 17.

> GABRIEL
>
> ..."Nicolas" has a second profile and is currently banging Geraldine and Julie. *And...* (with another photo) he and his Turkish mother are here illegally.

CLOSE on Snowden's eyes darting across the screen, thrilled and revulsed by his power to see lives like this before him.

> SNOWDEN
>
> That's it.

29.   INT. NIGHT CLUB - GENEVA - NIGHT

CLOSE on Matt shooting a local schnapps. CLUB MUSIC growls over loudly. Snowden looks out at the COCKTAIL WAITRESSES in thongs and pasties. TWO STRIPPERS dance on poles against the back wall.

SNOWDEN

What are we doing here, Matt?

Matt grins. Slings an arm around Snowden's shoulder.

MATT

You're making people very happy... Mr. Marwan's bank handles serious Saudi money. *And* a whole bunch of Russian billionaires.

SNOWDEN

What about Al-Qaeda money?

Matt ignores the question.

MATT

Ed: I'm up for a promotion soon. I won't forget my friends.

SNOWDEN

Thank you. This is all going pretty quick? I only sent you initial background...

MATT (looking past Snowden)

There he is! The man!

Snowden stands to shake his hand, but Marwan embraces him instead. Warmly, desperately.

SNOWDEN

Hey, Marwan!

MARWAN

Dave, how wonderful to see you.

SNOWDEN

Good to see you too.

MATT

Hey, I was counting, Marwan: you snuck
in an extra half hour back there.

As the GIRL comes by Marwan, a compliant smile.

MARWAN

I'm afraid she was merely tolerating an
old man's woes (sitting).

SNOWDEN

So how have you been, Marwan?

MARWAN

I must tell you, Dave--since we met, my
life has gone somewhat topsy-turvy.

SNOWDEN

I'm sorry to hear that.

MARWAN (nodding at Matt)

But your colleague, Charles, has
graciously offered his help. I owe him--
and you--a great deal.

Marwan grins, waves down a waitress and orders.
Snowden is trying to read some clue from Matt.

SNOWDEN

Can I ask what happened?

MARWAN (struggling)

My daughter...uh...

He can't go on. Matt puts a hand on his shoulder.

MATT

Marwan's daughter...took too many
sleeping pills. She's all right. It has to do
with her boyfriend who was deported
recently. We're trying to secure a visa
for him.

MARWAN (fighting tears)

Even so, I'm afraid that Salma... I'm
sorry. I won't trouble you with such
matters...

Drinks arrive. Snowden is staring at Matt in disbelief.

MATT

Talk as much as you want. Family comes
first.

Matt clinks Marwan's glass. With a look to Snowden.

30.   EXT. NIGHT CLUB - GENEVA - NIGHT

LOUD MUSIC BOOMS from the club as BOUNCERS open
the club doors for Matt and Marwan, who stumble out,
screaming and dancing.

Snowden follows after them, stone-faced, as they careen
down the sidewalk. Matt virtually carrying Marwan.

Marwan fishes out his keys, starts punching the UNLOCK
button in the direction of one car after another without
success.

MARWAN

Call back to me, my love!

Matt negotiates Marwan onto a bench and takes the keys.

Matt moves down the sidewalk, trying cars. Snowden glances at the slumped over Marwan and jogs after Matt.

SNOWDEN

What the fuck is going on?!

MATT

I've been acting swiftly and effectively on the very good signals intelligence you provided.

SNOWDEN

And if his daughter had died?

MATT

We could've worked with that too.

SNOWDEN

In the name of a promotion?

Matt bristles, lets it slide. A Mercedes BEEPS: Marwan's car.

MATT

Marwan can't be away from his family right now. So tomorrow morning, when he's facing a week in jail, we're going to offer him a deal and he won't turn it down.

SNOWDEN

Jail for what?

MATT

Drunk driving. Now I want <u>you</u> to call
the police. Say you saw a Mercedes
headed north--

SNOWDEN

He'll kill himself. He's not driving
anywhere.

MATT

OK. I'll call them.

Matt heads towards the car. Snowden blocks him.

SNOWDEN

He's <u>not</u> driving.

MATT

Remind me--are you authorized on
any of those NSA programs you used?
(Snowden is silent) See, we're all doing
fucked up shit.

Matt starts to move past him. Snowden puts his hands on
Matt's shoulders, stopping him.

MATT

Watch yourself, Ed.

SNOWDEN

I'll tell him who you are.

MATT

Oh? You reveal the identity of an
undercover officer and you're going to
jail for a lot longer than Marwan.

Matt walks on to Marwan's car. Snowden lets him go. He
looks back at Marwan trying to stand.

31.   INT. SNOWDEN'S APARTMENT - GENEVA - NIGHT

Ed undresses at a window overlooking the city. His eyes
wild--as if he's coming down off a drug. Lindsay stirs in
bed and awakens.

LINDSAY

Hey...

SNOWDEN

Sorry I'm so late.

LINDSAY

How was work?

SNOWDEN

It was all right. I have to wake up in
three hours. My flight's at seven.

He walks to bed and settles in. Lindsay slips a hand into
his boxers.

LINDSAY

Better be quick then.

Within moments, they're having sex. Ed is grateful to lose
himself. The escape almost brings peace to his face.

But as they're nearing climax, his eyes catch on Lindsay's open LAPTOP nearby. His body freezes as he fixes in on the laptop's small circle of glass.

MOVING IN on the eye of black glass, staring back at him. Until it fills the frame.

32.   INT. SNOWDEN APARTMENT - GENEVA - EVENING - WEEKS LATER

As Ed sits at his laptop nearby, splitting his looks between the TV and ARCHIVE FOOTAGE of a recent speech by Obama on his computer.

> **SENATOR OBAMA (on computer)**
> I will provide our intelligence and law enforcement agencies with the tools they need to track and take out the terrorists without undermining our Constitution and our freedom...That means no more illegal wiretapping of American citizens. No more ignoring the law when it is inconvenient. That is not who we are.

The door opens, and Lindsay enters with grocery bags. She wasn't expecting him to be here.

> **LINDSAY**
> Hi hon', what happened to the London trip?

> **ED**
> I'm not going.

LINDSAY (putting groceries away)

Oh? ...What's going on? Who's winning?

ED

It's still early.

Lindsay, out of the kitchen, goes to their shared desktop, sees on TV:

CORRESPONDENT (TV live)

...Exit polls from the battleground state of Ohio are looking good for Senator Obama... (continuing)

LINDSAY

Come on, big ears! Let's see how Florida's looking...

She sees an update on the computer.

LINDSAY

Holy shit, he's going to win it. You can act all nonchalant but I know you're starting to root for him. I've been watching your inner liberal grow. For which I'll take a modest percentage of the credit.

Lindsay's eye catches on a BAND-AID placed over the desktop's webcam. She peels it off, inspects it as Ed comes over, takes the band-aid, and reapplies it in the same place.

ED

Russian hackers. Agency says they can activate webcams now.

LINDSAY

That's creepy.

She returns to typing.

LINDSAY

Whatever. Let 'em look. It's not like I'm hiding anything.

Ed shakes his head cynically.

ED

That's such a bullshit line. 'I have nothing to hide.' Everyone has something to hide.

LINDSAY

Not me. I don't.

Lindsay stops typing as she sees Ed's face.

LINDSAY

What?

ED

OK. The other day your computer was open and I happen to notice that you were on the site that we met and you were looking at other guys.

LINDSAY

Oh you were just looking at my computer?

ED

I wouldn't have even brought this up.
You asked me 'what do I have to hide'
and that's something you're not telling
me.

Lindsay's been caught. She takes a breath, not seeking an
excuse.

LINDSAY

I don't do anything. I don't meet any
of those people. You're gone for weeks
at a time so it's like I'm peering into
other people's lives because mine is
temporarily on hold.

Ed considers her.

ED (stung)

Sounds like an excuse.

LINDSAY

It's the truth.

Lindsay tries to touch him. Ed is unresponsive.

LINDSAY

I should've told you and I didn't. I'm
sorry, but it's not a big deal.

She tries again. He starts to reciprocate.

LINDSAY

I don't want anyone else. I don't want
any other life. Okay?

They kiss tentatively, then more playfully.

ED

Listen...I didn't go to London today
because I resigned.

LINDSAY (stunned)

What?

ED

Personal differences...It was a matter of
principle.

LINDSAY

Can you tell me anything else?

ED

No.

LINDSAY

Does this mean you get re-posted?

ED (pause)

I resigned from the CIA, Lindsay.

LINDSAY

So, what do we do?

ED

I don't know. But this is a good thing.
Trust me.

LINDSAY

I do.

Lindsay sits beside him. Ed is watching the TV turns up the volume intently. Lindsay turns to see: Obama casting his vote in Chicago.

                          LINDSAY
          He's going to win.

                            ED
          He'd better.

Lindsay looks at him. A conflict in his eyes she doesn't understand. She puts a hand on his.

                                        CUT TO:

                     PRESIDENT OBAMA
          ...Every agency and department should
          know that this administration stands
          on the side not of those who wish to
          withhold information but of those who
          seek to make it known.

                                     CUT BACK:

33.   INT. SNOWDEN'S ROOM - MIRA HOTEL - HONG KONG #3A - NIGHT

Ewen and Glenn talk fast as Laura and Ed listen.

                       GLENN (V.O.)
          Janine is the website editor of a small
          stateside office of a British newspaper up
          against the most powerful government
          in the world. You have no idea what
          pressure they'll put under her.

EWEN (V.O.)

She won't be bullied. We <u>need</u> to establish that we're not compromising national security by publishing.

GLENN

We need to have alternatives.

Glenn moves closer to Ed:

GLENN

Look, Ed, the real issue here is that they-- the White House--are now aware that Janine has a leaked top secret FISA court order. Anything could happen. They could subpoena the *Guardian* and for that matter, they could come through this door any minute and end this entire thing. We must seriously think about doing this ourselves on our own website. We have no choice--

EWEN

You can't just start dumping documents on the Internet, Glenn! Be serious. Look what happened to WikiLeaks. It destroyed their credibility. Ed, you said it yourself: if this isn't done properly, the world won't pay attention. We need experienced journalists to walk the public through some very complicated stories.

GLENN

We are experienced journalists.

Snowden is divided, unsure. But as he's about to speak--
RING! RING! All four freeze, staring at the HOTEL PHONE
by the bed.

GLENN

Has anyone called before?

ED (concerned)

Not once. In three weeks.

EWEN

I suggest I answer it. Wrong room or...

Meanwhile Ed walks over and puts his hand on the
phone. He looks up at them:

ED

Yes? (beat) No, I don't. (beat) I will.

He hangs up, heads for the door.

ED

They asked if I wanted turndown
service. They said the 'Do Not Disturb'
sign wasn't on the door.

He opens it, sees the sign is gone, and with a quick frantic
search, finds it has floated down onto the floor of the
inside closet. A communal exhale as he hangs it back on
the door, and closes it, locks it...Pause, then the tension
returns quickly.

GLENN

So? Do we wait? Or go on our own?

Ed shakes his head--it's not his decision.

ED

I told you when we started, Glenn: how
you publish is your business, not mine.
I trust you. All I asked is that you study
the data and be responsible. No names.
No specifics. Anything ongoing that's
critical, do not release. Keep to the
issue of general surveillance and let the
people decide.

GLENN

You have our word on that, but that's
not the question.

Ewen, seeing where this is going, jumps in:

EWEN

Ed, the White House is setting up
a conference call for Janine with
intelligence officials now. It should
happen in the next few hours. Let's at
least wait for that. See what they say to
her.

Ed thinks it over...

ED (to Glenn)

Why don't we pause a moment?

Glenn relents, nodding.

EWEN

I suggest we reassemble here after the
call takes place. (looking at his watch)
Let's say sometime around midnight,
noon in New York.

GLENN

All right. I'll take another pass at the
PRISM story in the meantime.

END Laura's camera POV. Glenn and Ewen grab their
phones and head out.

EWEN (to Ed)

We'll be at our hotel if you need us.

Laura starts packing up her camera. As she removes his
wireless mic, she notices Ed staring at her camera. She
holds out the camera to him.

LAURA

Here--have a look, it might make you feel
better.

He takes it, turns it in his hands, as if it was a weapon...

LAURA

When did this start for you? Not wanting
your photo taken?

ED

Japan. Every time a camera was pointed
at me, it was like...I couldn't breathe.

LAURA

Why was that?

ED

I guess I spent too much time looking at
other people through cameras.

The look in Ed's eyes is haunted.

LAURA

Japan was your first NSA job, right?

ED (nods)

As a Dell contractor. With...a lot of access.

LAURA

Why'd you go back after Geneva?

ED

I went back for the money and 'cause I wanted to live in Japan.

He puts the camera to his eye, turns the focus.

ED

...and 'cause of Obama. I thought things would get better with him. I was wrong...

CUT TO:

34. INT. 5TH AIR FORCE, CYBER - YOKOTA AIR BASE - JAPAN - DAY

Following THREE INTELLIGENCE OFFICERS and FIVE high-level JAPANESE OFFICIALS down rows of computer stations--mostly AIR FORCE/NAVY PERSONNEL, in uniform, working at them. But the key elements are CIVILIAN CONTRACTORS.

SUPER: **Yokota Air Base, Tokyo - 2009**

SNOWDEN (V.O.)

At first, I was working on this round-the-clock back-up system called Epic

Shelter. If there was some catastrophe--
say, terrorists burned down every
embassy and NSA post in the Middle
East--this ensured we wouldn't lose any
of that data...

His expression darkens as the officers approach, asking
him something. The Japanese join, gawking as Snowden
pulls up for them a LIVE DRONE FEED, zooming in on: a
wedding in Pakistan.

SNOWDEN (V.O.)

But then I would have to put it aside
when visitors showed up. NSA wanted
to impress the Japanese, show them our
reach. They loved the live drone feeds.

CONFERENCE ROOM--US Officials on one side of the table,
pitching hesitant JAPANESE Officials on the other.

SNOWDEN (V.O.)

They weren't as thrilled to learn that
we wanted them to help us spy on the
Japanese population.

Snowden's monitor shows the busy central RAILROAD
STATION of Tokyo as he taps into a CCTV feed.

SNOWDEN (V.O.)

They said it was against their laws. Of
course, we tapped the entire country
anyway.

Snowden, at his station, types code while looking at a
second monitor showing a MAP OF JAPAN, indicating key
sites.

SNOWDEN (V.O.)

And we didn't stop there. Once we
owned their communications systems,
we started going after their physical
infrastructure.

MONTAGE of Japanese hospitals, power lines, stock
market.

SNOWDEN (V.O.)

We'd slip these little sleeper programs
into power grids, dams, hospitals. The
idea was: if the day came when Japan
was no longer an ally...

EXT. TOKYO--shots of power going out in the railroad
station and across the city.

SNOWDEN (V.O.)

...it'd be 'lights out.'

IMAGES of a darkened country. An empty train platform.

SNOWDEN (V.O.)

And it wasn't just the Japanese. We
were planting malware in Mexico,
Germany, Brazil, Austria... China, I could
understand. Russia, Iran, Venezuela?
Sure. But Austria?

CLOSE on his colleagues' cynical expressions across the
watch floor. Sharing his discontent.

Multiple scenes start POPPING out:

ARCHIVE FOOTAGE--Clips of the HEADLINES from the
2009-2011 period. Foreign elections, bankers, protests,
strikes, etc.

SNOWDEN (V.O.)

You're also being ordered to follow most
world leaders and heads of industry.

A succession of webcam POVs and text messages--
Politicians and Executives communicating sensitive
information.

News feeds of G8 / G-20 SUMMIT CONFERENCE
MEETINGS...UNITED NATIONS MEETINGS, etc.

SNOWDEN (V.O.)

...because you're also tracking trade
deals, sex scandals, diplomatic cables to
give the US an advantage in negotiations
at the G8, or leverage over Brazilian oil
companies, or helping to oust some third
world leader who isn't playing ball.

The frame is a collage of scenes now, all shrinking...

SNOWDEN (V.O.)

Ultimately, the truth sinks in no matter
what justifications you're selling
yourself: this isn't about terrorism,
terrorism is the excuse.

...until each scene is the size of a pixel, and the pixels
start to swirl, coalesce, becoming...

SNOWDEN (V.O.)

This is about economic and social
control, and the only thing you're
protecting is the supremacy of your
government.

...flickering points of light in Snowden's eyes.

35. **INT. SNOWDEN'S ROOM - MIRA HOTEL - HONG KONG #3B - NIGHT**

LAURA

Were you thinking about going to journalists then?

ED

No, it wouldn't have occurred to me back then. I still thought the system would self-correct. The president'd keep the promise that got him elected. That's when I remember reading about you and your films in Glenn's blogs. Being detained at airports for hours.

LAURA

Thirty-seven times! For investigating your own country's wars...(indicating her camera) That's why I'm going back to Berlin to edit. You can trust me with this.

ED (sadly)

I do, and I haven't trusted really anyone in...(thinking) years.

36. **INT. 5TH AIR FORCE, CYBER - YOKOTA AIR BASE - JAPAN - DAY**

Snowden is engaged by an INTEL OFFICER.

SNOWDEN (V.O.)

It was a welcome change when they put me onto terrorism watch duty. Every

day, I'd get starting points for SIGINT--
signals intelligence.

CLOSE on Snowden's monitor: a list of names and emails.

SNOWDEN (V.O.)

A lot of them were American. Which felt
strange, but you just keep reminding
yourself: *I could stop a dirty bomb
attack and save thousands of lives.*

Back on Snowden, overwhelmed. On his monitor: a world
map.

SNOWDEN (V.O.)

The thing is: you're not just following
your bad guy targets. You're also
following their metadata--all the phone
numbers they're in touch with.

A red dot appears on the map over Lebanon.

SNOWDEN (V.O.)

So let's say your target is a shady
Iranian banker operating out of Beirut...

A scene pops out of Lebanon: the BANKER, Skyping.
The scene keeps playing as lines start spreading from
Lebanon.

SNOWDEN (V.O.)

...so you start watching everyone he
talks to on a regular basis...

One-line goes to a red dot in upstate New York--a scene
pops out of Buffalo: office surveillance camera POV of a
DENTIST working over a patient's open mouth.

SNOWDEN (V.O.)

...including, you know, his cousin, who's
just some dentist living in Buffalo.

ZOOMING on Buffalo. Lines travel out across the city.

SNOWDEN (V.O.)

...then you have to watch who that
dentist talks to...

Another line from Buffalo goes to Miami, a scene pops
out--CCTV of a BARTENDER receiving selfies from the
dentist.

SNOWDEN (V.O.)

By the time you go a third 'hop' out from
your original target...

A scene pops out of Denver--a MOTHER, Skyping with the
bartender. The mother is pulling at the skin around her
eyes.

SNOWDEN (V.O.)

...you're watching a bartender chat with
her mother about botox.

The map EXPLODES with new scenes...Pulling back:
Snowden at his STATION. He looks anesthetized. Staring
at the JUSTIFICATION WINDOW in his XKeyscore
program. He punches in an image of the drop-down box
with "recently used justifications."

SNOWDEN (V.O.)

'Cause three hops from anyone with,
say, forty regular contacts, and you're
looking at a list of 2.5 million people.

The BANKER's Skype pops out again.

SNOWDEN (V.O.)

Then there's that moment when you're
sitting there and the scale of it hits you.

The frame is a collage of scenes now, all shrinking...

SNOWDEN (V.O.)

The NSA is really tracking every cell
phone in the world. No matter who you
are, every day of your life, you're sitting
in a database just ready to be looked at.

...until each scene is the size of a pixel, and the pixels
start to swirl, coalesce, becoming...

SNOWDEN (V.O.)

Not just terrorists, or countries, or
corporations...but you.

...flickering points of light in Snowden's eyes.

37.   INT. SNOWDEN'S ROOM - MIRA HOTEL - HONG KONG #3C - NIGHT

LAURA (delicately)

Was Lindsay with you in Japan?

ED

Japan was...difficult for us.

LAURA

I guess you couldn't talk about your
work.

ED

There was one night. Towards the end.
We were supposed to climb Mount Fuji
the next day...

38. INT. SNOWDEN'S APARTMENT - TOKYO, JAPAN - EVENING - 2009

In a compact, modern Japanese apartment low to the
floor, Ed wanders around the LIVING ROOM, packing
food, clothes into a backpack...Lindsay sits at her desk
with her laptop. The energy between them is fragile and
edgy.

He passes behind her, seeing her laptop; he stops. On the
screen is: a TOPLESS PHOTO of Lindsay in a yoga pose.

SNOWDEN

You going to post that on Twitter?

LINDSAY

No, they're just for me. What do you
think?

Lindsay clicks through a few more TOPLESS PHOTOS of
herself.

SNOWDEN

You should delete them.

LINDSAY

Not quite the artistic critique I was going
for.

SNOWDEN

You can't have stuff like that on your
hard drive.

LINDSAY

Yes, I can.

SNOWDEN

I'm asking you to please delete them.

LINDSAY

'Russian hackers' again?

SNOWDEN

No.

Snowden is silent. Lindsay studies him. Reading him.
Seeing the guilt. She stands and confronts him.

LINDSAY

Is it us?

SNOWDEN

It's classified.

LINDSAY

Am I a target?

SNOWDEN

Of course not.

LINDSAY

Clearly someone is looking at my nude
portraits.

SNOWDEN

I shouldn't have brought this up. There
are...issues of national security.

LINDSAY

I'm flattered that my boobs are
considered an issue of national security,
but you're going to have to do better
than that.

Snowden moves away, continues packing. Lindsay
pursues him.

SNOWDEN

I'd rather not talk about stuff that could
land us in jail.

LINDSAY

This is what the band-aids are about,
isn't it? And the camera phobia?
Because of your work? Are they
watching us? Who are they watching?

SNOWDEN

NO ONE! We're going to stop talking
about it. And we're going to go climb this
fucking mountain. OK?

LINDSAY

Of course we're not going to talk about it.

SNOWDEN

What's that supposed to mean?

LINDSAY

It means we don't talk about anything.
You work twelve-hour days. You come
home depressed. You play fucking video
games and then you fall asleep.

SNOWDEN

I'm tired. I have a job. That's how we pay
for an apartment in the most expensive
city in the world.

LINDSAY

Which you asked me to come to.
Knowing I didn't have a work visa.

SNOWDEN

And if you had one? Would you really
interrupt your life of eating, sleeping,
and socializing? Do you even want a
career?

LINDSAY

You mean do I want a career being
miserable--like you all the time?

SNOWDEN

That's called "responsibility".

LINDSAY

Fuck this.

SNOWDEN

You have no fucking idea what it means
to be accountable for other people's lives
because you live in a fairy-tale land

where there are no consequences and no
one ever gets hurt.

> LINDSAY

No, you don't get hurt. I get fucking
crushed.

> SNOWDEN

Fucking bullshit. I've done nothing to
you!

> LINDSAY

That's exactly right. You've done
nothing. You don't hang out with me,
you haven't laughed with me. You don't
even fucking touch me anymore.

Snowden moves toward her. She backs off.

> LINDSAY

No.

Lindsay goes into their bedroom. Shuts the Japanese
screen. Snowden sits at their desktop, very hurt.

39.   INT. SNOWDEN'S ROOM - MIRA HOTEL - HONG KONG #3D - NIGHT

CLOSE on Ed remembering...

> SNOWDEN

We never made it to Mount Fuji. Lindsay
left. It was lonely. After three months, I
went back to Maryland. I promised her
I'd changed.

40.   EXT. LINDSAY'S PARENTS' HOUSE, MARYLAND

Snowden stands at the front door, shifting nervously, as Lindsay opens it from the inside. For a moment, it looks like she might slam it in his face again. Then she wraps her arms around him.

> SNOWDEN (V.O.)
>
> We moved in together...

41.   INT. POLECATS FITNESS STUDIOS - MARYLAND - DAY

CLOSE on a woman's bare back arching. Fingers reaching. A naked leg moving up a pole.

Lindsay, in spandex and sports bra, is teaching pole-dancing to 12 OTHER WOMEN, students who practice around her, as she makes adjustments.

She smiles, surprised, when she sees Ed watching her through the window.

> SNOWDEN (V.O.)
>
> When you're really happy, there's a large part of you that just wants to stay happy...

42.   EXT. POTOMAC RIVER & NATIONAL MEMORIAL, D.C.

Snowden and Lindsay sitting on the banks of the river on a beautiful day. He's putting a simple gold chain bracelet on her...they walk pass the Teddy Roosevelt Monument.

SNOWDEN (V.O.)

You start to think: what could be more
important than this? Lot's of people
cruise happily through life, Why can't I?

INT. SNOWDEN'S ROOM - MIRA HOTEL

SNOWDEN

And I went back to work for the CIA.

INT. CIA CONFERENCE ROOM -- a DOZEN IC MEMBERS
watch Snowden in a suit giving a power point. They seem
impressed.

SNOWDEN (V.O.)

My official title was Solutions
Consultant. Basically I was hawking
overpriced hardware for a living.

INT. SNOWDEN'S ROOM - MIRAA HOTEL

LAURA

I thought you'd resigned?

SNOWDEN

It was all contract work after Geneva.
Dell or Booz Allen Hamilton partnered
with CIA, NSA, DIA. The intelligence
community's 'revolving door'.

LAURA

How was is it? Being back in the States?

SNOWDEN

It was good to be home. But...

Snowden's expression goes grim.

SNOWDEN

> Maryland was where things started to
> turn for me...

INT. HOUSE, MARYLAND -- NEAR DAWN. Snowden, his
laptop open. Lindsay asleep next to him.

SNOWDEN (V.O.)

> ...Every time I felt like I was finally
> letting go of all the anxiety, all the
> questions that used to keep me up at
> night...

Snowden sees something on the internet.

SNOWDEN (V.O.)

> ...I would learn something more that I
> just couldn't ignore.

Snowden leans forward, engaged by ARCHIVE FOOTAGE
from 2007 (five years prior) of THREE MEN, 50s/60s. A
caption reads: Former NSA Officials' Homes Are Raided
by FBI.

SNOWDEN (V.O.)

> Like there were these three high- level
> officials at the NSA. Bill Binney, Ed
> Loomis, and Kirk Wiebe. They'd been
> filing complaints about abuse and
> overreach for years.

FOOTAGE from local news and national shows
(*Democracy Now*, etc.) of Bill Binney and the others
following the raids on their homes.

SNOWDEN (V.O.)

That's all they did. They filed
complaints. And the FBI raided their
homes.

INT. SNOWDEN'S OFFICE, MARYLAND -- Snowden at his
desktop, watches a clip from *60 Minutes*. As host, SCOTT
PELLEY, introduces the subject of his show: NSA whistle-
blower, THOMAS DRAKE, 57.

SNOWDEN (V.O.)

And then there was Thomas Drake... and
like those three other guys, Drake tried
to change things from the inside. When
nothing worked, he did go to the press.

On Internet: ARCHIVE FOOTAGE of Drake headed to
court.

SNOWDEN (V.O.)

So they hit him with the Espionage
Act. We were shocked. The whole intel
community.

On Internet: Scott Pelley is sitting down with Drake.

SCOTT PELLEY

Why do you think you were charged?

THOMAS DRAKE

To send a chilly message.

SCOTT PELLEY

To who?

THOMAS DRAKE

To other whistle-blowers and to others in
the government not to speak up. Do not
tell truth to power, or we will hammer
you.

43.   EXT. HUNTING PRESERVE - MARYLAND - DAY

CLOSE on two pairs of knee-high rubber boots moving
through a marshy ground. MISHKA, a black labrador,
bounds between them, disappearing up the far bank.

Snowden trudges after her up a hillside of beech trees.
Beside him is: Corbin O'Brian...Both wear camo jackets,
orange vests, and hunting bag belts. They carry 20-gauge
double barrel shotguns.

SUPER: **Maryland - 2011**

O'BRIAN

...There's a new program being
developed at NSA's op center on Oahu.
You'd be going up against cyber divisions
in the Chinese military. Interested?

O'Brian notices Snowden seems more reserved than
usual.

O'BRIAN

It wouldn't be the vast sums you're
making now. But you'd be performing a
critical service for your country. I know
that's important to you.

SNOWDEN

You mean 'service' like in Geneva?

O'BRIAN

Matt was a mistake. I shouldn't have
pushed you into that.

SNOWDEN

You didn't. I wanted exposure to field
ops. You gave it to me. I don't hold that
against you.

O'Brian catches a note of disenchantment. They've
reached the edge of a field. Twenty yards off, they see
Mishka frozen peering at the bush ahead. She doesn't
turn back.

O'BRIAN

...Is there something you do hold against
me?

SNOWDEN (looks, pause)

...You didn't tell me we were running a
dragnet on the whole world, Corbin.

O'Brian let's it go and walks past Snowden.

Suddenly, BARKING and FLAPPING...TWO PHEASANTS
come shooting out of the brush less than 12 feet away.
Snowden spins and FIRES. The first drops. He tracks the
second further down the field. FIRES. A tiny BURST of
feathers.

O'BRIAN

Great shooting, Ed. That's terrific!

SNOWDEN

That's one thing I was good at in the
army.

As they head for the downed birds.

                    O'BRIAN

Y'ever think Ed--since the Second
World War, it's been 60 years, and still
no WW3? Why? Because we've used
our power generally for the good of the
world. For prosperity. Order. How can
we defend ourselves against nuclear
war, terrorism, cyber attacks without a
centralized intel factory working around
the world night and day?

                    SNOWDEN

So we should catalog people's lives?

                    O'BRIAN

People already catalog their lives for
public consumption.

                    SNOWDEN

Parts of their lives. By choice. We're not
giving them the freedom to choose. And
we're taking everything.

                    O'BRIAN

Most Americans don't want freedom.
They want security.

Mishka locates the second pheasant deep in the brush, 20
yards off...They approach.

                    O'BRIAN

This is a simple bargain: if you want to
use all the new toys and be safe, you pay
the price of admission.

SNOWDEN

Except people don't even know they've
made that bargain.

O'BRIAN

Where is the modern battlefield, soldier?

Snowden hesitates. Then repeats the classroom answer:

SNOWDEN

The battlefield is everywhere.

O'BRIAN

What is the first rule of battle?

SNOWDEN

Never reveal your position.

O'Brian moves beyond the classroom, asks a new
question:

O'BRIAN

And if one unauthorized person knew
our position? If Congress knew?

SNOWDEN

So would the enemy.

O'BRIAN

That, Mr. Snowden, is the state of the
world. Secrecy is security. And security
is victory.

44.   EXT. HUNTING LODGE - MARYLAND - LATE AFTERNOON

The party--TWELVE MEN, all top Intelligence Community members--has gathered before a HUNTING LODGE. They drink, chat. Most are old friends.

> O'BRIAN
>
> Someone I want you to meet.

O'Brian directs him toward: TIMOTHY LOWELL, 58. Lanky, hawk-nosed, currently the NSA's deputy director. The most powerful man in this group.

> LOWELL
>
> How'd you make out today, Corbin?

> O'BRIAN
>
> Very mediocre. Nothing like Ed here. Apparently the Army is training people to shoot straight.

> LOWELL
>
> So this is Ed Snowden.

Snowden shakes Lowell's hand, uncertain why the deputy director knows his name.

> LOWELL
>
> The brains behind Epic Shelter.

> SNOWDEN (surprised)
>
> Yes sir, thank you.

> LOWELL
>
> It's brilliant work.

O'BRIAN (to Lowell)

You know it's proving very useful to our
UAV program.

LOWELL

Yes, I heard. With foreign site intel
transfer.

Snowden hasn't heard anything about this. He listens,
confused at first. Then starting to catch on:

O'BRIAN

Transfers happen on collection now.
Goes straight to Langley, Pentagon,
Mossad if they need it. Actionable
immediately. No one sees it. It's
improved the response time of our drone
pilots by a factor of ten.

Lowell turns to Snowden, who's stunned.

LOWELL

Tell me, Ed: You worked signals
intelligence in Japan too, yes? How'd
you like it?

SNOWDEN

It's an...empowering job sir.

LOWELL (chuckles)

With this new job in Hawaii, you'd have
even more access. I asked Corbin to
start the conversation. But the offer is
mine.

Snowden is still processing the news about Epic Shelter.

LOWELL

Take your time. It's going to take a few
months to get this program on its feet.
If you'll excuse me, gentlemen, I see
dinner.

Lowell heads toward a BUFFET TABLE where pheasants
are now being served. Snowden turns to O'Brian, who
sees his unease.

SNOWDEN

Corbin, Epic Shelter was meant as a
back-up program.

O'BRIAN

Lowell is creating this position for you,
Ed. You'd be the very first contractor
deployed outside Fort Meade working
counter-cyber... It's your ticket to the
top.

Snowden follows him toward the buffet grill where the
pheasants are being grilled.

45.   INT. POLYGRAPH ROOM - CIA HEADQUARTERS - LANGLEY, VA - DAY

CLOSE on a laptop showing FOUR GRAPHS of oscillating
lines. Snowden has been fitted with chest and finger
sensors as before. A POLYGRAPH ADMINISTRATOR
studies the graphs as they unfold.

POLYGRAPH ADMINISTRATOR

Do you believe the United States is the
greatest country in the world?

> ### SNOWDEN (after a pause)
> Yes.

The line skews. The Administrator notes it.

> ### POLYGRAPH ADMINISTRATOR
> Have you ever used any programs you
> weren't authorized for?

> ### SNOWDEN
> No.

Another ANOMALY in the lines. The administrator also notes it.

46.   INT. ED & LINDSAY HOUSE - MARYLAND - NIGHT

CLOSE on Ed, deep in thought, chopping carrots at the counter. Lindsay is measuring and re-sizing her self-portraits.

> ### LINDSAY
> ...We're not supposed to submit our own
> work, but my editor said she'd make an
> exception. Sweet, right?

Ed isn't listening. Lindsay walks to the kitchen counter to try to get his attention.

> ### LINDSAY
> I get to submit an entry...you ignoring
> me on purpose?

ED

Sorry...(he stops chopping) I was going
to talk to you about it at dinner...

LINDSAY

Is everything okay?

Ed pulls Lindsay into the living room and sits her on the
couch.

ED

The deputy director of the NSA offered
me a new position. That was a while back
and now they need an answer.

LINDSAY

...Is it something you want?

ED (equivocating)

I'd be good at it.

LINDSAY

Can you tell me anything about it?

ED

You know I can't.

LINDSAY

Yeah sure--"Mission first." How about
social perks? White House galas maybe?

ED

The position's in Hawaii.

LINDSAY (disappointed)

Ed, things are just starting to click. We have <u>real</u> friends. I have a job I actually <u>like</u>. Our parents are here. And you're willing to rip it all up again? After all the work we put in?

ED

I understand and if you want to stay, we're staying. That's it.

LINDSAY

Don't just say that cause I want to hear it.

ED

I'm not. I let you go once. I'm not doing it again.

Lindsay feels he means it. She quiets. Ed spots the pot of water on the stove boiling over.

ED

Oh, the pasta!

He turns the burner down, testing the pasta inside.

ED

Hey, I actually think I got it close to right this time.

LINDSAY

I'll get some candles.

She goes down the hall. Ed pours the pot of pasta into a strainer. The steam making his eyes blink.

ED'S POV: fuzzy with the steam. Too fuzzy. He shakes his
head. The sound of SOFT BELLS. Where is this coming
from?

His POV--the pasta receding as if down the drain. The
bells louder. Too loud. Inducing vertigo.

Ed suddenly falls. His POV of a ceiling fan. Lindsay
returning. Her mouth moving. No sound. Only the bells.

From LINDSAY'S POV--kneeling beside him, pasta
everywhere. His body trembles. His eyes vacant. She lifts
his shaking head, bleeding slightly from the fall.

> LINDSAY
>
> Ed?

47.   INT. DOCTOR'S OFFICE - MARYLAND - DAY

Ed sits before a FEMALE DOCTOR, 40s, writing out a
prescription. Lindsay beside him.

> ED
>
> I know Tegretol. It slows you down. My
> mom's tried all sorts of drugs her whole
> life. She still has seizures.

> FEMALE DOCTOR
>
> They work in 70 percent of cases. Ed:
> epilepsy is a serious condition. If you
> have a seizure driving yourself--or
> with someone else in the car (looks at
> Lindsay), or you're in a place where
> you could fall, this is not something to
> be lightly regarded. It's essential you
> commit to this medication...Ok?

Lindsay looks at him. Sees him nod. She squeezes his hand.

48. INT. EXPLORER - PUBLIC PARKING LOT - LANGLEY - SAME DAY

Lindsay opens the car door for Ed.

> ED (small smile)
>
> Thank you.

Lindsay climbs into the driver's seat and watches him, concerned.

> LINDSAY
>
> Ed, I was thinking about what the doctor said, about the stress. A warmer climate could help. If Hawaii is something that we decide would be better for you--I'll go.

49. EXT./INT. SNOWDEN'S ROOM-MIRA HOTEL-HONG KONG #4-NIGHT 1AM

LONG SHOT of the hotel window in the distance. The shadows of the journalists and Snowden--pacing.

Janine's face in a video chat window on a laptop. It's 1PM New York time, DAYLIGHT outside.

Ewen, Glenn, and Laura are huddled around the laptop.

> EWEN
>
> Janine, how'd the White House conversation go?

JANINE

I made it quite clear we were in
possession of an authentic FISA court
order. They wanted to see it. We refused.
Now I just pray it's actually authentic...

GLENN

Are you actually questioning that?

JANINE

Glenn: no one's ever seen a FISA court
order. There's no precedent here.

GLENN

Our source risked his life for that
document! It's real. Tell us, did the
White House raise any specific national
security concerns that would prevent
you from publishing?

The question hangs in the air. A lot riding on it.

JANINE

No. I asked them repeatedly and they
had no substantive answer.

GLENN (not surprised)

Then, there you go! What more do you
want? You can go out and know that
you're safe.

JANINE

Glenn, I'd like to talk to Alan before we
go any further.

(Left to right) Lindsay Mills (Shailene Woodley) and Edward Snowden (Joseph Gordon-Levitt) in Hawaii.
Photo credit: Mario Perez

(Left to right) Trevor James (Scott Eastwood) and Edward Snowden (Joseph Gordon-Levitt) at a NSA facility in Hawaii. **Photo credit:** Jürgen Olczyk

(Left to right) Director Oliver Stone with Scott Eastwood (as Trevor James) on the set of SNOWDEN. **Photo credit:** Mario Perez

(Left to right) Edward Snowden (Joseph Gordon-Levitt) and Lindsay Mills (Shailene Woodley) in the home they share in Hawaii. **Photo credit:** Mario Perez

(Left to right) Oliver Stone and Joseph Gordon-Levitt (as Edward Snowden) on the set of SNOWDEN.
Photo credit: Mario Perez

Laura Poitras (Melissa Leo) prepares to interview Edward Snowden.
Photo credit: Jürgen Olczyk

Laura Poitras (Melissa Leo) in the Hong Kong hotel room.
Photo credit: Jürgen Olczyk

Glenn Greenwald (Zachary Quinto) in the Hong Kong hotel room.
Photo credit: Jürgen Olcyk

(Left to right) Laura Poitras (Melissa Leo), Edward Snowden (Joseph Gordon-Levitt), Ewen MacAskill
(Tom Wilkinson) and Glenn Greenwald (Zachary Quinto) in the Hong Kong hotel room.
Photo credit: Jürgen Olczyk

(Left to right) Edward Snowden (Joseph Gordon-Levitt) and Lindsay Mills (Shailene Woodley) in Washington, DC on their first date. **Photo credit:** William Gray

(Left to right) Director Oliver Stone, Joseph Gordon-Levitt (as Edward Snowden) and Shailene Woodley (as Lindsay Mills) on the set of SNOWDEN. **Photo credit:** William Gray

(Left to right) Edward Snowden (Joseph Gordon-Levitt) and Lindsay Mills (Shailene Woodley) near the White House in Washington, DC. **Photo credit:** William Gray

EWEN

When does he land?

STUART

In six hours.

GLENN

No! No! Absolutely not! We're sitting
ducks here, Janine. It's 1PM New York.
If you don't get this posted in the next
four hours, you will miss the evening
news on the East Coast.

JANINE

We can post later tonight...(pause)
Glenn, I'm sorry. Alan's our editor in
chief, and I really think--

GLENN (losing it)

THIS IS BULLSHIT. THE GOVERNMENT
KNOWS WE HAVE THESE DOCUMENTS
NOW AND THE CIA COULD BARGE
DOWN THIS DOOR ANY MINUTE AND
YOU WANT MORE TIME?! ACT LIKE A
JOURNALIST AND STOP STRINGING US
ALONG!

Ed motions to Glenn, and Laura waves to keep his voice
down, indicating the walls and ceiling.

JANINE (hurt)

I just stood my ground with the
goddamn White House! I've risked my
career! How dare you question my
commitment to this story!

EWEN

Come on now. Let's lower our voices
here.

GLENN

You're right I'm questioning it! What
you're doing is not acceptable. We are
publishing ourselves! You are out!

Janine is close to blowing up, looking at Stuart.

Laura and Ewen look at Glenn, surprised at his
harshness. Even Glenn recognizes the difficulties of his
demand.

JANINE (a deep breath)

All right, Glenn. We'll have this ready by
4PM. We need to go over the story once
more.

GLENN

Why?

JANINE (exasperated)

Because it still needs editing, damn you!
All this fucking intelligence jargon is
hurting our brains. This PRISM story is
still incomprehensible.

GLENN (tart)

PRISM is the second story, Janine...You
have 24 hours to fix that. Verizon is the
first story. Have it ready to post by 4PM,
5 the latest! No games or we're gone.

He punches a key. The chat goes dark. A taut silence follows, their looks ending on Ed, who looks at his watch, tense as well. This is definitely a bump in the road.

CUT TO:

50.   EXT. THE TUNNEL, NSA OPERATIONS CENTER - HAWAII - DAY

Snowden's POV--up a wooden flight of stairs from a PARKING LOT ending at a giant, circular ENTRANCE built into a hillside with foliage. Covered by an awning, it looks ordinary, but it's deceptive--it's open to the elements without a doorway, like a WWII bunker. There is a rundown GUARD SHACK next to the entrance.

SUPER: **'The Tunnel,' NSA Ops. Center, Oahu, Hawaii - 2012**

51.   INT. THE TUNNEL - HAWAII - DAY

REVERSE on Snowden, once he's inside, looking back 30 yards at the entrance described from the other side. On the inside of it is an ordinary electronic CHECKPOINT.

> SNOWDEN (V.O.)
> So my new job was counter spying on the Chinese at the NSA Regional Cryptological Center in Oahu.

Snowden turns a corner and moves into a Turnstile, swiping his RFID CARD, nodding to TWO SECURITY GUARDS.

GUARD #1

No laptops, no USB sticks, no cell
phones, no electronics of any kind...?
(Snowden nods) Ok. Go ahead.

He steps into a PLEXIGLAS MAN-TRAP, which closes
behind him, a BLINKING RED LIGHT above him. GUARD
#2 puts his backpack on an X-RAY SCANNER's conveyor
belt. Guard #1 POV--of Snowden--skeleton, etc. The light
goes GREEN. The second door opens. Snowden steps out,
collects his backpack.

52.   INT. THE TUNNEL - HAWAII - DAY

Snowden walks on downward to a giant elevator, studying
his new home from a pocket map, we hear:

GABRIEL (V.O.)

'Snow White'! Is that you?

Snowden surprised to see GABRIEL SOL from Geneva.

SNOWDEN

Gabriel!

GABRIEL

Dude, what the hell are you doing here?

SNOWDEN

You work here?

GABRIEL

Yeah. Three years, two months, five
days, but who's counting?

Snowden nods as they walk to a giant elevator where
15 OTHER PERSONNEL wait. Ahead of them we note
a large open WORKSPACE (1st Deck). The majority of
personnel, 60 percent of 1,000, are in uniform, Navy, Air
Force, some Army--but a significant 40 percent are NSA/
CIA civilians or contractors in casual clothing--some flip-
flops and shorts, with hoodies for the icy air conditioning.
Some shuttle in GOLF CARTS. Snowden and Gabriel
continue on to the freight elevator.

> ### GABRIEL
>
> Who knew a secret, underground World
> War Two airbase'd become munchy
> heaven for a thousand geeks?

> ### SNOWDEN
>
> So there's good pizza?

> ### GABRIEL
>
> Yeah, good pizza. Elevator is slow as shit
> though.

> ### SNOWDEN
>
> What deck you on?

Gabriel ignores the question.

> ### GABRIEL
>
> You NTOC ('en-toc')? Or ROC ('rock')?

> ### SNOWDEN
>
> Between you and me? NTOC.

GABRIEL

Cool. You get to hack the hackers.
Coming up in the world.

They get in the elevator. The giant doors close.

53.   INT. NTOC - 3RD DECK - TUNNEL - DAY

SUPER: **NATIONAL THREAT OPERATIONS CENTER**
-- the station door is opened from the inside by TREVOR
JAMES, early 30s. Crew cut. The competitive zeal and
ambition of a West Point graduate.

GABRIEL

Fresh brains for you Trevor.

Trevor looks coldly at Gabriel and gives Snowden a firm
handshake.

TREVOR

Trevor James. Interactive Ops Division
Chief.

SNOWDEN

Ed...Snowden.

TREVOR

I've been briefed.

Snowden enters a decked-out ROOM with THREE
CUBICLES--each a workstation with three chairs and
monitors for each chair. There's about eight personnel per
shift (24-hour operation). A large WALL SCREEN, rear
projected, looms over the space.

TREVOR

Next door is NTOC, defense. That's
where you'll be working. Over here we
have ROC, our offense. I move between
the two. We run a tight ship here,
Snowden.

SNOWDEN

Yes, sir.

TREVOR

You'll be working with Haynes.

Another occupant of his cubicle is PATRICK HAYNES,
mid 20s. He approaches Snowden, shakes his hand.

PATRICK

Patrick Haynes. Good to have you.

GABRIEL (re: Patrick)

Watch out for him--he's the smartest guy
in the building. How many languages
you speak again?

PATRICK

Seven coding, six spoken, two sign.

Snowden signs to Patrick. (BOLD indicates subtitles.)

SNOWDEN

I know some ASL.

PATRICK

(surprised, signing back)

No shit! That's awesome.

TREVOR

Just what I need: another language I can't understand (closing the door on Gabriel).

GABRIEL

I'll check you later, Ed.

54.   INT. ROC CENTER (REMOTE OPS), 3RD DECK-TUNNEL, HAWAII-DAY

(30 MINUTES LATER)

JSOC PREDATOR DRONE CAMERA POV--of cement buildings in a mountainous DESERT. A group of FIGURES exits a building, starts down a street. Impossible to tell their age or sex.

TREVOR

Wait for it. Any moment...

A FLASH OF LIGHT replaces the figures.

TREVOR

Lights over Waziristan, gentlemen.

Trevor, Snowden, and Patrick are watching the drone's live feed on the flat screen. The room is similar in design and style to NTOC with three cubicles, eight personnel per shift. But the hardware is devoted to hacking, not counter-hacking.

Smoke clears over a CRATER, Snowden sees Patrick's ambivalent expression. Trevor is eating an energy bar.

SNOWDEN

What do we contribute to this?

TREVOR

Underside of that Reaper drone is
fixed with a big-ass antenna, snarfing
the hardware IPs of everything that
broadcasts. We do the geolocating,
and my buddy at the Air Force rains
hellfire... (opening a VIDEO CHAT
window) There he is...

AIR FORCE DRONE PILOT

Enjoying the fireworks, Trev?

TREVOR

You know it. We Track 'Em, You Whack
'Em.

The DRONE PILOT chuckles and gets back to work.
Trevor leaves the video chat window open but puts his
friend on MUTE.

SNOWDEN

So...Who did we just track there?

TREVOR

Not who. What. We're targeting the bad
guys' cell phones. Sometimes the SIM
card.

The drone POV is scanning over charred BODY PARTS.

SNOWDEN

How do we know that the bad guy is in possession of the bad cell phone when we strike?

PATRICK

We don't.

TREVOR

Of course we do. JSOC and CIA have their people in the field.

PATRICK (signing to Snowden)

He's full of shit. He doesn't know.

SNOWDEN

What's the program name?

TREVOR

Epic Shelter. Originally some back-up program for...(looking to Patrick) what was it...

SNOWDEN

"Catastrophic Site Failure."

TREVOR

Yeah. How'd you know?

SNOWDEN

I built it.

Trevor looks at him with new respect. Snowden capitalizes on the moment:

SNOWDEN

You know, I've been thinking about
another use for Epic Shelter.

TREVOR

What'd you have in mind?

SNOWDEN

I was chatting to Jim Lowell, and--

TREVOR (even more impressed)

Deputy Director Lowell?

SNOWDEN

We were talking about how there are so
many programs it's impossible to keep
track of them anymore. Why not create
a centralized database?

PATRICK

Like an index?

SNOWDEN

Yeah, that updates in real-time. We've
already got *Epic Shelter* collecting our
finished intel, we just need a web portal
to catalog it, make it searchable.

TREVOR

Let me think about it...In any case I'd
have to run it by Fort Meade. Did you
have a name?

SNOWDEN

If it's not taken, I'd like to call it
Heartbeat.

Trevor takes the video chat with the drone pilot off mute.
CLOSE on Snowden. A new intensity in his eyes.

AIR FORCE DRONE PILOT (V.O.)

Engage target.

An eerie silence follows as we pull back on Snowden and
see he's not looking at the drone feed anymore. He's
looking at...

55.   EXT. MOUNTAINSIDE - HAWAII - DAY

...Ed hiking a steep mountain trail. Breathing hard.

SUPER: **Oahu, Hawaii - 2013**

He looks up: ahead, Lindsay's reached the top of the
mountain. She's pointing her camera at him. He pulls his
arms up, covering his face.

LINDSAY

Come on! It's been years...By social
media standards you don't even exist
anymore.

Sighing, he raises his hat. Lets her take the photo.

LINDSAY

Gotcha. The elusive E, captured.

ED

Am I a viable boyfriend now?

LINDSAY

It's a shame: you used to be such a cute
little model...

ED

Little?

Ed joins her at the summit, starts tickling her. They take
in the magnificent view together: the verdant island, the
sea beyond.

LINDSAY

I never thought I'd say this, but I think
you got some sun.

ED

Impossible.

LINDSAY

I've been meaning to ask you: did you
switch pharmacies? Because I tried to
pick up your medication and I couldn't.

ED

Why would you do that?

LINDSAY

I was just...there and I thought I'd ask.

ED

I stopped taking the Tegretol.

LINDSAY (shocked)

What? When?

> ### ED
>
> A couple of months ago.

> ### LINDSAY
>
> And you're just telling me this now?

> ### ED
>
> I've been meaning to. I can't take that stuff. It makes me groggy and I need to be sharp for work.

Lindsay, pissed, starts packing up her camera.

> ### LINDSAY
>
> What is it about this fucking job that makes it more important than your life?

> ### ED (after a pause)
>
> Our government is...hemorrhaging billions of dollars a year to Chinese hackers. I've been hired to shut them down. A lot of people are depending on me.

Lindsay is suspect but allows herself to buy the white lie.

> ### LINDSAY
>
> More so than anyone else?

> ### ED
>
> Yes.

LINDSAY

We didn't come here for you to heal, did
we? There never was a 'less stressful
job' in Hawaii.

ED

I feel like I'm made for this. If I don't do
it--I'm not sure who else can...(looking
back down the trail) I'm on a trajectory I
can't turn back from.

As Lindsay starts heading back down the mountain:

LINDSAY

You can always turn back.

Ed hurries after her.

56.   INT. 3RD DECK - CAFETERIA - THE TUNNEL - DAY

Snowden gets coffee to go, and joins a GROUP OF
ANALYSTS tensely looking up at the TV monitors
available in the space. Gabriel and Patrick are already
there as Snowden joins.

On TV--a clip of CSPAN footage: a US Senate Intelligence
Committee. Senator Ron Wyden hearing testimony from
the director of National Intelligence, James Clapper.

SENATOR WYDEN

Could you give me a yes or no answer
to the question: Does the NSA collect
any type of data at all on millions, or
hundreds of millions of Americans?

DIRECTOR CLAPPER

No, sir.

Some Analysts drift away mumbling, unsurprised. On screen:

SENATOR WYDEN

It does not?

DIRECTOR CLAPPER

Not wittingly. There are cases where they could...inadvertently, perhaps, collect...but not wittingly.

GABRIEL (whispers)

Oh really?

The gears are turning in Snowden's head. Something more than mere disgust on his face...

57.   INT. NTOC - 3RD DECK - TUNNEL - DAY

Patrick, Gabriel, and Paul 'CATFISH' Cafferty, 30s, tattooed, congenial, with a hippie vibe, are watching Snowden, typing.

SNOWDEN

I came across this working on a new indexing program...

A WORLD 'HEAT' MAP appears on his flat-screen. Color-coded countries. A heading reads: BOUNDLESS INFORMANT. They stare at it. This is new to them.

GABRIEL

What is this?

SNOWDEN

Data collection worldwide for the month
of March. Emails and Skype calls.

He types: number box appears next to France.

SNOWDEN

France: 70 million. Germany... (with
more boxes) 500 million. Brazil: two
billion.

A US number box appears. It reads: 3,095,533,478.

SNOWDEN

In one month, NSA collected 3.1 billion
calls and emails from **inside the United
States**...and that's a partial count, it
doesn't include any Telecom company
data.

Their expressions: stunned.

CATFISH

Fuck me. What's the collection in
Russia?

SNOWDEN (pulling it up)

1.5 billion.

PATRICK

We're collecting twice more in the US
than we are in Russia?

CATFISH

I figured it was a lot but...

GABRIEL

Shit is out of hand, man.

CATFISH

Have you shown this to anyone else?

SNOWDEN

No. You're the first.

PATRICK

I'd be careful about showing that around.
Could look like you're rocking the boat.

SNOWDEN

I'm just curious to know if I'm the only
one who thinks this is crazy...

Their faces are the answer. He's not.

The door swings open--and Trevor appears. He freezes
when he sees Gabriel, Catfish--and the Heat Map.

TREVOR

What the fuck is going on? (to Gabriel
and Catfish) What're you doing in here?

A taut moment as Snowden responds.

SNOWDEN

It's cool, Trevor. (struggling) I was just
showing them this slide... I wanted their
input.

TREVOR

Why the 'Heat Map'?

CATFISH (jumping in)

It's my bad, Trev. I made a bet with Ed about which country we're collecting the most signals from. He said Iran, I said Pakistan.

TREVOR

Who won?

CATFISH

Ed.

Trevor stares at Gabriel who exits, Catfish following him.

GABRIEL

I need to head out. I'll see you guys.

Catfish hands Snowden a 20-dollar bill.

CATFISH

You're going down next time.

Trevor, cold, closes on Snowden.

TREVOR

No more bets. And I don't want anybody unauthorized in here again. Especially not with the *Heartbeat*.

SNOWDEN

You're right. Won't happen again.

58.   EXT. SKY OVER NEIGHBORHOOD - HAWAII - NIGHT

QUAD COPTER NIGHT-VISION POV: down on streets and rooftops of an upper-middle-class SUBURBAN NEIGHBORHOOD. A low BUZZING.

Hovering over: a BLUE HOUSE with a BARBECUE FIRE in the backyard--Friends from Lindsay's show and Colleagues from Ed's job in two separate groups. Lindsay's birthday cake lies mostly eaten on a table...One of Ed's colleagues is controlling the drone as others set off small FIRECRACKERS, which light up the scene for the drone.

59.   EXT. BACKYARD - ED & LINDSAY HOUSE - HAWAII - NIGHT

Sitting around the fire are: Ed, Patrick, Gabriel, Catfish, and OTHERS on the team from the Tunnel drinking beers. Ed, at the edge of the group, abstains.

Ed looks through the flames at Blake and Lindsay finishing the birthday cake, chatting in the SECOND GROUP on the porch. He senses the energy between them, his envy stirring...SOUND returns as we pick up Catfish in mid-story:

CATFISH

> ...this blurry object wanders into the strike zone. We all knew it was a kid...Poof--he's gone. We called for clarification. Report came back: it was a dog.

The Group falls quiet. Not a fun story at all!

CATFISH

...Okay. But the same village, two,
three days later, we see the funeral
party. About 15 of 'em. Moms and Dads
wailing...The order comes down clear--
'hit 'em'...(whispering) Poof! And
they're gone in a cloud of dust. All of
'em-- the whole fucking family (pause)...
The crazy thing is you come home after
work, kiss the wife, kids, back to work
next day. Pretty soon, it all becomes
routine.

Ed shares a look with him. Feels the deadness.

TREVOR

Fuck that. You make it sound criminal
man! It's war, it's a job.

CATFISH

I don't know...Jobs can't be criminal?

TREVOR

Not if you're working for the
government.

ED (suddenly)

You've heard of the Nuremberg Trials,
Trev? They weren't that long ago.

TREVOR (wary)

Yeah. And we hung the Nazi big shots,
didn't we? So?

ED

That was the first trial. The next one
was guards, lawyers, policemen, judges.
People who were just following orders.
That's how we got the Nuremberg
principles, which the UN made into
international law... (pause)...in case
ordinary jobs become criminal again...

Trevor coolly glances at Ed, wondering where this
is coming from...One of the fireworks hits the QUAD
COPTER, which comes crashing down with a flurry of
noise in the backyard, breaking up the mood.

Ed steps away, looking through a window at Lindsay
making a drink for Blake in the house...The image goes
fuzzy.

Ed shakes his head. BELLS start. As before. Louder.
Darkness converges. Ed suddenly terrified, looks at
the fire--a flicker at the end of a tunnel. The bells are
SCREAMING now.

TIME CUT -- Lindsay running out of the house. Ed's
colleagues calling her, frantic. Ed is lying on the ground,
trembling in a partial seizure. She turns him on his
side. Puts his shaking head in her lap. Trevor watches,
worried.

His POV: the face of Lindsay and his friends speaking with
no sound. Far away...

60.   INT. COMMUNICATIONS ROOM - 1ST DECK -
       THE TUNNEL - DAY

Snowden is in a low-lit room. He's alone, unsure of what's
coming. The WALL-SCREEN is lit up with the image of:

Corbin O'Brian, via a secure link from his Langley office.
Standing before him, Snowden is a fraction of his size.

                        O'BRIAN

        Hey, Ed. How are you? How's your
        health?

                        SNOWDEN

        Fine, thanks for asking.

                        O'BRIAN

        Must be nervewracking--living with that
        condition. You wouldn't know it looking
        at your numbers: two hundred Chinese
        IPs down in your first four months!

                        SNOWDEN

        Those are internal numbers.

                        O'BRIAN

        Your colleague, Trevor, comes out of
        the CIA like you. (Snowden didn't know
        this) He's been keeping me informed on
        your progress. It's outstanding work.
        Heartbeat as well.

                        SNOWDEN

        Thank you.

                        O'BRIAN

        Lowell is very pleased. He sends his
        regards (pause)...He doesn't know
        about...your heat map conversations--or
        some of the ideas you've expressed to
        your colleagues. And he's not going to.

A pause. The purpose of O'Brian's call is clear now.

SNOWDEN

Heartbeat's proving tricky-- collating
from multiple agencies, knowing what
to grab. It helps to talk it over with
colleagues.

O'BRIAN (scrutinizing him)

I believe in you, Ed. Which is why
nothing happened to you after the derog
in Geneva.

SNOWDEN

I'm very grateful for you looking out for
me.

O'BRIAN

Or after you...'omitted the truth' on your
last polygraph. What was it you were
withholding exactly?

SNOWDEN
(ignoring the question)

Do you remember that day in class,
when you taught us about the FISA
court? You said they'd approved Bush's
wiretapping program.

O'BRIAN

Sometimes we're restricted from telling
the whole truth. That doesn't give us
permission to lie.

SNOWDEN

Corbin, the director of National
Intelligence just lied to Congress!

Snowden turns away, trying to swallow his anger.

O'BRIAN

Look at me.

Slowly, Snowden looks up. O'Brian's giant eyes are
magnetic. In spite of himself, Snowden's captivated by
them. Made vulnerable.

O'BRIAN

Did you access an unauthorized
program?

Snowden hesitates, knows this is the ball game. Throwing
up his hands as if to say: *you win.*

SNOWDEN

Yes. In Geneva. It was Lindsay. I was
<u>jealous</u>...I'm sorry. I <u>never</u> did it again.

A long beat. Those eyes. Then O'Brian nods, as if he
understands.

O'BRIAN

I know it's been up and down for you
and Lindsay since Geneva... It's tough
to keep any relationship going. Few of
us do...(Snowden nods in agreement)
So, if it'll give you any peace of mind, I
can assure you: she's not sleeping with
her photographer friend--if that's what
you're thinking. I'm going to a 'Five

Eyes' conference in Sydney in a couple of
weeks. I'll stop off in Hawaii. Okay?

SNOWDEN (pause)

Okay...thank you.

As he nods compliantly, pretends to be reassured.
Corbin's motive in revealing this is ambivalent to him--
both paternal and threatening.

O'BRIAN

I'll see you soon.

As he vanishes into the black screen, Snowden is rooted
in the empty room, his mind reeling with the implications
of what he's just heard.

61. EXT./INT. ED & LINDSAY'S HOUSE - HAWAII - DAY

Ed rushes home and approaches Lindsay sitting at her
desk just as she takes a call on her cell.

LINDSAY

Hey, Dad. Did you get those photos?

She walks past Ed giving him a quick kiss as she
continues down the hallway. Ed moves his gaze to her
laptop on the table. He enters. He sits at the laptop and
starts typing. A PGP KEY GENERATOR opens on the
screen.

He keeps typing until: Lindsay appears.

TIME CUT -- Lindsay putting a hand on his shoulder.

LINDSAY

What are you doing?

Ed, sitting in her chair at the table, closes the laptop. He stands, puts a finger to his lips. An intensity in his eyes that Lindsay's never seen.

Ed calmly motions for her to put her phone on the table. Lindsay obeys, Ed's demeanor putting her on edge.

Ed motions for her to follow him out the front door... Halfway down the driveway, he turns to her, addressing her in a low voice:

ED

Your email's being monitored.

LINDSAY

So?

ED

This is different, this is not passive collection. You're a target of full-take surveillance now. Social media. Text messages. Calls. Everything. It's possible the house is bugged, I'm not sure.

Lindsay senses that he's telling the truth. But is also wary of him right now--he's not on the Tegretol anymore...

LINDSAY (rattled, confused)

By who?

ED

By a senior officer at the CIA.

LINDSAY

Are you in trouble? Is it the Chinese
thing?

ED

There are things I wish I could tell you--
but I can't, because you could get very
hurt. What's keeping you safe right now
is that you don't know anything. The
more you know, the more danger you'll
be in.

Lindsay looks shaken, afraid.

ED

I'm so sorry, Lindsay. I truly am. I
didn't want this for you...But I know
you'd think I was doing the right thing.
(pause) Now listen to me closely: when
we go back in that house, we're going
to behave as if nothing has changed.
Everything we do has to appear normal.
If you notice anything strange--people
following you--I want you to tell me
immediately using the encrypted email
account I'm setting up for you.

Ed waits for some sign of acknowledgment.

LINDSAY

Jesus Christ, Ed...I don't know if I can do
this...

ED

Yes, you can. I know you can.

LINDSAY

Do I even have a choice?

ED

I'm asking you to trust me.

He reaches out to embrace her but she pulls back. It's
a spooky moment for Lindsay. She sees how far along
this mystery path he's traveled. Her fear mixed with
resignation now.

ED

And Linds: I think it would be a good
idea if you went back to Maryland.
Tell your parents I'm going away on
a business trip and you're feeling
homesick.

LINDSAY

Are you going away?

ED

Just for a little while.

LINDSAY (thinking it over)

No. I'm staying here.

ED

Please. At least until I return--

LINDSAY

You said our behavior has to appear
normal. If both of us left at the same
time wouldn't that seem suspicious?

She's right and they both know it. Ed nods slowly. Lindsay heads up toward the house, then turns back to him:

LINDSAY

I'll do this for you. But it's the last time.

Unmoving, Ed watches her walk into the house. The finality in her voice driving home the true sacrifice of what he's about to do.

62.   EXT./INT. ED & LINDSAY HOUSE - HAWAII - NIGHT

In a corner of their yard, Ed has set up his laptop and connected it to a YAGI ANTENNA and SIGNAL AMPLIFIER.

He sits in the dark, lit only by his screen, staring at a program called Kismet.

CLOSE on the screen as he scrolls down 50 surrounding Wifi networks available to him via the Yagi. He selects one. Opens an email window. Closes his eyes. Breathes.

In the message window he types: *We will meet in the mall, opposite the Mira Hotel, on the Monday two weeks from now. I will be holding a Rubik's cube.*

63.   INT. 3RD DECK - THE TUNNEL - DAY

Gabriel sees Snowden coming in, spinning a Rubik's cube-- the one from Hank. He looks deeply preoccupied.

GABRIEL

You hear about Trevor, bro? (off Ed's confused look) Check this out.

Snowden follows. Gabriel stops near the ROC. On the other side of the glass, Trevor is talking with a GROUP OF TAO (Tailored Access Operations)--all Navy ensigns in uniform.

We can't hear the conversation, but it's clear that Trevor's chewing them out and doing a very thorough job.

GABRIEL

Remember that op to 'own' the Internet in Syria? Trevor and his TAO team bricked the core router. Whole country's gone dark.

SNOWDEN

Holy shit...

As they watch Trevor start laying into the youngest ensign:

GABRIEL

Poor bastards...

SNOWDEN

I gotta get back to work.

Snowden heads for the NTOC, Gabriel watches him.

GABRIEL

Hey, Ed. How's Heartbeat coming?

SNOWDEN

Close...very close.

Gabriel nods, a knowing look in his eyes.

64. INT. NTOC - 3RD DECK - TUNNEL - DAY

Snowden enters spinning his Rubik's cube. Patrick is
there, shuttling hurriedly between multiple monitors of
code.

SNOWDEN

Don't tell me you're involved in this too.

PATRICK

Trevor fucking roped me into going
through their zero-day exploit code...See
why it failed...Thing's a mess...

Trevor makes eye contact with Patrick, waves at him
urgently.

PATRICK (groaning)

Why did I agree to this?...

Patrick stands, heads out of the NTOC.

SNOWDEN

Good luck.

Snowden watches Patrick join Trevor. He sits at his
workstation. Keeping one eye on Trevor, he pries the top
off his Rubik's cube, and furtively removes a MINI SD
CARD. He installs it in a drive.

On his monitor, he opens the HEARTBEAT folder.
There are now dozens of organized folders of slides and
documents inside.

They have names like: domestic surveillance, false
testimony, constitutional violations, FISA Amendments
702, executive orders. He drags folders to the card, starts
to copy them...

His face, tense but calm looking around at the heads
of passing Personnel outside his cubicle; they can't see
much.

Snowden's POV of Trevor: a NAVY COMMANDER arrives.
A whole group of officers with him. Trevor quickly goes
from scolding the ensigns to getting torn apart himself.
Snowden smiles.

Snowden pops the SD card out and installs a second card
into the drive. When that starts copying he carefully,
quietly, inserts the first card back into his Rubik's cube.
Again it all seems quite normal in the flow of the room.

CLOSE on Snowden's 'copying' bar edging closer to
completion. He pulls it out and puts a third one in.

Snowden's POV: Trevor's verbal beating continues. He
looks completely miserable. Nodding and stammering.
The Commander points back to the NTOC, toward
Snowden. Trevor and Patrick start heading toward him.

Snowden has to hurry now...

CLOSE on Snowden's 'copying' bar reaching 100 percent.
Snowden hears the sound of their voices and snatches
the SD card out just in time. But he's too rushed...

When he tries to insert the card into the Rubik's cube, he
applies too much pressure and the card goes spinning out
of his fingers, landing on the carpet, half-way to the door.
Just as: Patrick opens it.

TREVOR (V.O.)

This is bullshit, man! Talk about getting
held out to dry.

Patrick follows Snowden's eyeline to the card. Grasps the situation immediately and then stands on it as Trevor enters. Patrick glances at Snowden; it's hard to say what he's thinking--but then he turns to Trevor.

SNOWDEN

Trouble with the Navy?

TREVOR

One of those idiots ripped some bullshit piece of Israeli code and jammed it into our payload. Can you fucking believe that?

SNOWDEN

Script kiddies.

TREVOR

I know, I know...I should've listened to you. Goddamit...(to Patrick) Is this it?

Trevor is pointing to a chunk of code on Patrick's monitor. Patrick nods. Trevor quickly copies the code onto a drive.

TREVOR

I am not taking the fall for this.

Trevor heads out with the drive. Patrick lifts his shoe off the SD card and turns to the door as Snowden picks it up.

SNOWDEN

Patrick--(signing) **I might not see you again.**

PATRICK (signing back)

**You're going to leave me alone with
Captain America? Thanks a lot.**

Snowden smiles.

SNOWDEN

The NSA may come after you.

PATRICK

**I don't know what you're talking
about.**

They share a long look. Nothing more needs to be
communicated. As Patrick leaves, Snowden a little
nervously, inserts the SD card in his Rubik's cube.

65.   INT. 3RD DECK - HAWAII

A FEW MINUTES LATER-- Snowden sets out across the
floor, more Navy personnel now. He nods to some familiar
faces, working his Rubik's cube. His heart thumping. The
elevators seem a mile away and eyes seem to linger on
him. He spots Gabriel ahead. They make eye contact and
intersect.

GABRIEL

Headed home already?

SNOWDEN

Yeah, not feeling so good. Doubt I'll be in
tomorrow either.

They share a look.

                              SNOWDEN

Trevor's kind of busy, maybe you could
let him know for me?

                              GABRIEL

It would be my pleasure.

They reach the elevators.

                              GABRIEL

You know, if you're really not feeling
well, maybe you should go back to the
States and see your doctor. I think folks
would understand that.

                              SNOWDEN

That sounds like a smart thing.

Snowden steps into the elevator. They look at each other
warmly as the elevator closes.

66.   INT. TUNNEL - HAWAII - DAY

SECURITY CAMERA POV-- Snowden approaching the
MAN-TRAP. Two Guards alongside notice him coming.
As he works his Rubik's cube with both his hands, totally
absorbed.

One of the Guards sees him, now accustomed to his habit.

                              SNOWDEN

Hey, you ever play with one of these?

Snowden casually tosses the cube to Guard #1.

                              GUARD #1

Yeah, when I was a kid.

Snowden smiles warmly and places his backpack on the
conveyer belt and is about to step into the MAN-TRAP.

> ### SNOWDEN
> You should try it. It's hard.

SCANNER POV--Snowden's skeleton. Various colors on it.

His POV- Guard #1 is pointing out the Rubik's cube to
Guard #2. Saying something. They look at him. Snowden
quietly looks away, expecting trouble. The light goes
green. He walks out...Guard #1 hands him back the cube,
smiling.

> ### GUARD #1
> No way, man! Love these things! Have a
> good weekend.

> ### SNOWDEN
> You too.

Snowden takes his backpack and walks on...His heart is
beating noticeably to us as he sees the last 30 yards he
has to walk to the end of the Tunnel--daylight streaming
from outside. There's one more GUARD GATE at the
entrance.

EXT. TUNNEL--Snowden steps out into the fresh lush
green air of the island. His best moment in years.
Freedom.

67.   INT. SNOWDEN'S ROOM - MIRA HOTEL #5 - NIGHT/DAY

SILENCE. A CAULDRON of anxiety. Anticipation.
Uncertainty. Glenn still checking his watch...Ed going to
the window as NIGHT turns to DAY--VFX.

Laura at a laptop. She refreshes the *Guardian*'s website.

LAURA

It's <u>LIVE</u>!

Glenn and Ewen rush to her side. Snowden holds back. On the *Guardian* page, a new headline reads:

NSA Collecting Phone Records of Millions of Verizon Customers Daily Exclusive: Top Secret Court Order Requiring Verizon to Hand Over All Call Data Shows Scale of Domestic Surveillance Under Obama.

LAURA

There's a link to the FISA court order.

EWEN

<u>Well done</u>, Janine! (to Glenn) I told you she wasn't a pushover!

GLENN

...And it feels so goddamn good to be wrong!

Snowden at the laptop, eyes fixed to the screen. As he absorbs the story, he finally exhales, relaxes, satisfied. Ewen claps him on the shoulder. They're all still a little stunned that it happened.

TIME CUT:

Hours later the tension continues, draining them.

Glenn turns up the volume on the opening credits for CNN's *Piers Morgan Tonight*. The face of the newscaster appears. All their eyes peeled.

PIERS MORGAN

Breaking news tonight--reports that
through a secret court order the Obama
administration is collecting the phone
records of millions of Verizon customers.
That's been reported by the *Guardian*
newspaper in the UK. The specific court
order shows that all the information is
going to the National Security Agency...

The journalists cheer. Ed smiles.

LAURA

Not too bad for mainstream media, huh,
Glenn?

EWEN

They can't shut this down now. And we
have four straight days of it.

GLENN

They have no idea what they're in for.

68.   TIME CUT -- MONTAGE -- LAUNCH -- FOUR DAYS / FOUR NIGHTS

The pace picks up as we see ARCHIVE FOOTAGE--TV
and Web--NEWS ANCHORS in US and across the world.
Include Hong Kong, Australia, France, Germany, names,
files, pictures.

INTERCUT: Ed, Laura, Ewen, and Glenn tracking the
coverage through four days and nights / the journalists
running in and out of the room / Ed placing pillows by the
door each time--increasingly on edge about room security.

INSERT - TV - Glenn appearing on a PRISM interview in
Hong Kong.

> ### GLENN (ON TV, V.O.)
>
> He reached the conclusion that what was
> happening inside this really secretive
> agency was very threatening and
> menacing to privacy rights, to internet
> freedom, to basic political liberty not
> only in the United States but all around
> the world. And he felt it was his duty as
> a human being to disclose it.

TV NEWS -- ARCHIVE and SOUNDBITES continue of US
politicians and world leaders speaking out against the US
programs.

69.   INT. SNOWDEN'S ROOM - MIRA ROOM - HONG KONG #6A -DAY/NIGHT

Ed, Laura, and Glenn are exhausted, sleepless, still
immersed in the endless coverage--now including the
outrage from CONGRESSIONAL LEADERS on TV and
social media.

70.   INT. HOTEL ROOM - HONG KONG #6B - DAY/NIGHT

The actual Snowden sits in front of the TV, the image of
himself reflected in his glasses.

> ### SNOWDEN (CNN)
>
> ...My name's Ed Snowden, I'm 29 years
> old, I work for Booz Allen Hamilton as
> an infrastructure analyst for NSA in
> Hawaii.

Snowden's interview seems to be the biggest news of all! They have a face now! He watches himself on French, German, Chinese, Japanese stations.

SNOWDEN (V.O.)

You can't come forward against the world's most powerful intelligence agencies and be completely free from risk because they're such powerful adversaries. No one can meaningfully oppose them. If they want to get you, they'll get you in time.

INT. VIRGINIA HOME -- HANK, retired, feels to the contrary. His career is complete.

INT. WASHINGTON D.C. DEN -- Corbin O'Brian is furious. It's going to cost him. A phone rings off screen...

SNOWDEN (V.O.)

It's gonna get worse with the next generation and the next generation who extend the capabilities of this sort of architecture of oppression, you realize that you might be willing to accept any risk and it doesn't matter what the outcome is so long as the public gets to make their own decisions about how that's applied. Because even if you're not doing anything wrong you're being watched and recorded.

INT. PARENTS HOUSE (MARYLAND) -- Lindsay with, presumably, her Parents and a Friend, shocked, lonely-- but she understands now what happened.

SNOWDEN (V.O.)

I had access to the full rosters of
everyone working at the NSA, so if I
just wanted to harm the US? You could
shut down the surveillance system in an
afternoon. But that's not my intention. I
think for anyone making that argument
they need to think, if they were in my
position living in Hawaii, in paradise,
and making a ton of money, 'What would
it take to make you leave everything
behind?'

Ed watches the interview in silence and relaxes with a
long breath.

SNOWDEN (V.O.)

The greatest fear that I have regarding
the outcome for America of these
disclosures is that nothing will change.
And the months ahead, the years
ahead it's only going to get worse until
eventually...a new leader will be elected,
who flips the switch, and the people
won't be able to do anything by that
point to oppose it. And it will be turnkey
tyranny.

Glenn puts a hand on his shoulder. They're all concerned
for him.

GLENN

How you holding up?

Ed stands, MUTES the TV.

ED

I'll be fine. You guys have to start
watching after yourselves now.

Ed opens one of his laptops, starts typing.

ED

If you have any reason to believe that
you're about to be raided or intercepted,
or breached in any way, destroy
your data immediately. You have the
encrypted backups.

With a final stroke, he hits return.

ED

I no longer have access to any of the
documents myself. You have it all.

He looks back at his face on TV.

ED

Keep the focus on the stories. That's all
that matters. Now if you'll excuse me
(pause).

GLENN

Why don't we all get some rest. We need
it.

ED

Yeah, I think I can use some while I still
have a soft bed available.

71.   EXT. HONG KONG HARBOR - HONG KONG #7A - NIGHT

A LONG VIEW of the Mira Hotel. Dawn breaks. Snowden sleeps.

72.   EXT. BEACH - HAWAII - SUNSET

Lindsay and Ed face each other. Lindsay searches him. Ed stares at the sand. The surf. Paradise. Anywhere but her eyes which are daggers in his heart.

> ### LINDSAY
> Can you at least tell me where you're going?

Lindsay understands that she won't get an answer out him.

She takes his glasses off delicately and wraps her arms around him. Rocking him, turning in place.

> ### ED (constricted)
> Lindsay, I...

> ### LINDSAY
> Shh...

Without his glasses, the world seems different in her arms. As he turns, we see the traces of his tears. They dance against the sunset tender in each others arms.

73.   INT. LOBBY - GLENN'S HOTEL - HONG KONG #7B - MORNING

Glenn steps out of the elevator with his backpack on, cell phone to his ear. Ahead he sees A CROWD OF

JOURNALISTS. He slides deftly into the RESTAURANT/
BAR AREA.

GLENN

Shit. They're all over the place. No, I
don't see Tibbo--

Glenn's eye spies TWO MEN in suits conferring in the
lounge.

GLENN

Yes. Got 'em! I don't know. I'll figure
it out. I'll stop them with a press
conference...

Glenn hangs up, walks over carefully to the Two Men:

As they talk--a JOURNALIST spots Glenn, approaches.
The Two Men now move away. Glenn turns to face the
onslaught of Journos.

CUT TO:

74.   INT. SNOWDEN'S ROOM - MIRA HOTEL - HONG KONG #7C - DAYTIME

Ed, cleanly shaven, is putting in his contacts. There's
a KNOCK at the door and he opens to Laura and Ewen
who rush in and turn the TV on with Ed's face and the
headline: The Search for Edward Snowden.

ED

Did you get them?

From a plastic bag, Laura produces TWO PRESS PASSES
on lanyards. Hands them over. The laminate is coming
off.

LAURA

Best I could do. You're meeting Tibbo in
five minutes on the skybridge opposite
the large mall.

Ed hangs one around his neck. He puts on a baseball hat
without the glasses and he looks lightly disguised. He zips
up his bag.

Ewen clasps his shoulders warmly, for a Scotsman--

EWEN

I've met a lot of astonishing people in my
life, but you... (breaks off) Okay, laddie,
off you go...

Ed reacts shyly, self-consciously turns to Laura. She stops
filming and embraces him.

LAURA

We won't let you down.

She takes out the SD card and gives him the camera.

LAURA

You'd be a shitty journalist without a
camera.

ED

That's a great idea. Thanks.

Ed smiles and heads to the door when Laura notices his
Rubik's Cube on the counter.

LAURA

(holds the cube out towards Ed) You
don't want to leave your luck behind.

ED

I think I'd like you to have it. Thanks for
everything.

LAURA

Thank you.

INTERCUT:

CORRIDOR--Cautiously, he slips into the long passageway,
checking both sides, and goes crisply.

He seems to blend into the maze of low ceilings, shadowy
light, and mirrors that mark this peculiar hotel. Laura
watches him go.

VFX-- To her POV, Ed is reflected in the mirrors first as
two images--then four, then eight, 16--and then finally
some form of infinity...

**75.   INT. SKYBRIDGE - MIRA HOTEL - HONG KONG
         - MORNING**

POV down through glass at a CROWD OF JOURNALISTS
and TV TRUCKS making their way toward the Mira's
front doors.

Canadian barrister ROBERT TIBBO, 40s, watches from
the bridge between hotel and shops. We recognize Robert
as one of the men Glenn spotted in the lobby of his hotel.

Snowden in his baseball hat and sunglasses approaches
fast. They shake hands and hurry away.

76.   EXT. STREET - HONG KONG - DAY

Snowden and Tibbo rush towards a parked black sedan.

WE HEAR THE CRUSH OF MEDIA VOICES running over
BRIEF NEWS CLIPS.

REPORTER #1 (V.O)

The NSA leaker, Edward Snowden,
has now been charged formally with
espionage, theft, and conversion of
government property. US Officials have
asked Hong Kong to detain him on a
provisional arrest warrant.

REPORTER #2 (V.O.)

Snowden has checked out of the luxury
hotel in Hong Kong where he had been
holed up.

REPORTER #3 (V.O.)

The Justice Department had to go to
Interpol so that Snowden, if he tried to
cross a border, could be intercepted and
detained.

77.   EXT. MONGKOK DISTRICT - HONG KONG - SAME DAY

The sedan negotiates the loud, crammed streets of one
of Hong Kong's poorest areas, home to refugees and
immigrants.

REPORTER #4 (V.O.)

The Americans are now closing in. They
almost certainly know where he is, they
just need Hong Kong's approval to get
him.

REPORTER #5 (V.O.)

The Hong Kong government does
have an extradition agreement with
Washington...

The sedan idles by a Tong Lau Building--tenement
housing. Tibbo and Snowden slide out of the backseat.

78.   INT. TONG LAU BUILDING - HONG KONG - DAY

Tibbo and Snowden climb through a dark, filthy stairwell
filled with REFUGEES.

REPORTER #6 (V.O.)

But the big question here is: Where is
Edward Snowden?

They wear secondhand sweatsuits and sneakers, and
have darker skins than the Chinese, and unlike them,
they smile a lot, with dazzling white teeth.

Tibbo stops at a doorway and knocks. A MOTHER
wearing a sari opens the door, and Snowden enters a tiny,
dilapidated, TWO-ROOM APARTMENT--one room directly
next to the other, each filled by a mattress. SEVEN
PEOPLE live here. The kitchen is essentially the sink,
the toilet a hole in the ground with a sheet over it. The
furniture is plastic. TV doesn't work, no light.

The FATHER sits on a mattress with a BOY, two, and a
GIRL, five. His BROTHER and his WIFE and their CHILD
are in the other room, but they're moving out to give
Snowden their mattress. Ed's embarrassed.

Tibbo talks with the Mother and Father, who nod.
Ed finds a place on the mattress, the Kids watching
him pull out a portable YAGI ANTENNA and SIGNAL
AMPLIFIER, connecting them to his remaining laptop.

Tibbo approaches, sees the concern in Ed's eyes. With a Canadian accent:

TIBBO

...These are good people. They won't talk. Believe me, they have no love for the authorities. I've been handling their cases for years...Like you, they're stateless.

The eyes of the Seven People--not bitter or sad; on the contrary, they're grateful to be here.

TIBBO (indicates)

We're waiting on the UN application for refugee status. But just in case you're arrested...(giving him a card, gently) This is where you'll call.

SNOWDEN

Thank you so much.

TIBBO (about to exit)

You may not feel it Ed, but you're not alone.

With a warm smile, he departs. Ed faces the refugee family. The Mother smiles and indicates some tea. He smiles 'yes.'

TIME CUT -- FIVE DAYS LATER - NIGHT -- Ed sits on his mattress, feeling very alone. The VOICE of a NEWSCASTER on his computer:

NEWSCASTER #1 (V.O.)

His longtime girlfriend, Lindsay Mills, an amateur photographer, has not

been heard from. It's believed she's
in seclusion in her parents home in
Maryland and has been questioned
by the FBI and remains under
investigation.

TIME CUT -- IMAGE: TV COMMENTATOR to his news host.

The words bore Ed as he switches again to Lindsay's
website. But again it reads: This blog has been taken
down...He dozes off, heavy of heart.

TIME CUT -- FIVE MORE DAYS-- A VOICE comes over his
computer, but he continues to doze; he listens remotely,
stubble on his face.

NEWSCASTER #2 (V.O.)

Ten days have now gone by as the world
looks for Edward Snowden. Rumors
have surfaced that a rich supporter is
hiding Snowden somewhere in the Hong
Kong hills in a private mansion. But this
cannot be verified...

CLOSE on a little toe reaching out and touching his
shoulder, startling him from his reverie. The six-year-old
Sri Lankan Girl smiles. She hands him his glasses.

79.   INT. HONG KONG INTERNATIONAL AIRPORT - DAY

MONTAGE--WORLD NEWS--As Snowden, in disguise,
makes his way through the airport.

We hear many VOICES wash up against them like ocean
waves on a shore. A jumble of FACES and NEWS CLIPS
follow.

VOICE #1 (V.O.)

...now confirmed that Edward Snowden has boarded a flight from Hong Kong to Moscow...

VOICE #2 (V.O.)

...State Department very disappointed with authorities in Hong Kong for letting Snowden go...

VOICE #3 (V.O.)

...He was accompanied by a representative from Wikileaks...

VOICE #4 (V.O.)

...Snowden is trying to make his way from Russia to Cuba, and then to Ecuador for political asylum.

VOICE #5 (V.O.)

...Moscow airport officials say he won't be permitted to make his connecting flight because the US government has revoked his passport...

VOICE #6 (V.O.)

...The United States Secretary of State, John Kerry, outraged that Russia is refusing to arrest the American fugitive...

VOICE #7 (V.O.)

...now a man without a country, stranded inside the Moscow airport.

PRESIDENT OBAMA

...but no, I'm not going to be scrambling jets to get a 29-year-old hacker.

VOICE #8 (V.O.)

The president of Bolivia's plane was forced down in Austrian airspace today, following US suspicions that Snowden may have been on board.

VOICE #9 (V.O.)

...after 39 days in the airport hotel, he's left with his Russian lawyer and a legal advisor from Wikileaks--Sarah Harrison.

VOICE #10 (V.O.)

...he can now enjoy all of the sweet, sweet liberty allowed under the regime of President Vladimir Putin...

DONALD TRUMP (V.O.)

...there is still a thing called execution...

SARAH HARRISON

...Mr. Snowden actually deserves asylum and protection around the globe, but he does have asylum in Russia, at least. He can engage in the debate he started, and the world now has an example that you can do the right thing, and you don't have to end up in a cage, one room, a prison...

VOICE #11 (V.O.)

...after more than a year in the country
under temporary asylum, Edward
Snowden has received a three-year
residency permit in Russia.

80. EXT./INT. RUSSIAN APARTMENT - LIMBO

In a small place, Snowden is setting up three-point
lighting and a green screen (8x4). He has a camera and a
computer to self-record. He sits for the interview.

81. INT. AUDITORIUM - LIMBO

A little ROBOT rolls silently onto the stage on two wheels.
Affixed to it is a metal stand with a SCREEN.

The robot makes its awkward way towards center stage.
We see the screen now: Snowden's face. The bot turns,
looking out at a LARGE AUDIENCE, which applaud him
politely.

SNOWDEN

Forgive me if I get my bearings here.
People always said I was kind of a robot
(the audience laughs).

TIME CUT -- The MODERATOR remains unseen, a
distinguished voice.

MODERATOR

How is it you came to be in Russia?

SNOWDEN

Well, I never intended to end up here.
My passport was pulled en route to
Latin America. When people say: Why

are you in Russia? I say: ask the State
Department.

MODERATOR

Does that mean you're willing to go back
and face trial?

SNOWDEN

Absolutely, if it was a fair and public
trial. Unfortunately, that's not what
would happen right now, as long as the
Espionage Act is being used against
whistle-blowers.

MODERATOR

Do you still think it was worth it?

SNOWDEN

Yes, I do. Without the information
to start a public debate, we're lost...
The people being able to question our
government and hold it accountable--
that's the principle this country was
founded on. So if we want to protect
our national security, we should be
protecting that principle.

MODERATOR

What if your argument falls on deaf
ears? What if our leaders don't act?

SNOWDEN

I believe, if nothing changes, more and
more people around the world will come
forward. Whistle-blowers, journalists,

but also regular citizens. And when
those in power try to hide by classifying
everything, we will call them out on
it. And when they try to scare us into
sacrificing our basic human rights, we
won't be intimidated, we won't give up,
and we will not be silenced.

MODERATOR

You're alone in a foreign country, you'll
be extradited if you try to leave--that
must be hard...

Ed, in his small room, looks for the most honest
expression he can find for his feelings. He's not the Ed he
once was.

SNOWDEN

When I left Hawaii, I lost everything. I
had a stable life. A stable love. Family.
Future. And I lost that life, but I've
gained a new one and I'm incredibly
fortunate. And I think the greatest
freedom that I've gained is the fact that
I no longer have to worry about what
happens tomorrow, because I'm happy
with what I've done today.

MODERATOR

Live from the Internet...Edward
Snowden!

The audience breaks into sustained applause, which
turns into a standing ovation across the auditorium...
And in his small room Ed watches the response, humbled,
exhausted, but content--he's done all he can....

SUPER: **As of this date, Snowden resides in Moscow. Lindsay Mills has moved there to join him.**

CREDITS ROLL